KNITS IN A DAY

40 Quick Knits to Cast On and Complete in Three Hours or Less

Candi Derr

STACKPOLE BOOKS

Guilford, Connecticut

Published by Stackpole Books
An imprint of Globe Pequot
Trade Division of The Rowman & Littlefield Publishing Group, Inc.
4501 Forbes Boulevard, Suite 200, Lanham, Maryland 20706

Distributed by NATIONAL BOOK NETWORK
800-462-6420

Model and project photography by Daniel Shanken.
All other photos provided by the designers.

British Library Cataloguing in Publication Information Available
Library of Congress Cataloging-in-Publication Data

Names: Derr, Candi, 1973- editor.
Title: Knits in a day : 40 quick knits to cast on and complete in three hours or less / [compiled by] Candi Derr.
Description: Lanham : Stackpole Books, an imprint of Globe Pequot, Trade Division of the Rowman & Littlefield
    Publishing Group, Inc., [2017] | Features designs by Sarah Sundermeyer and others.
Identifiers: LCCN 2017018882 (print) | LCCN 2017019645 (ebook) | ISBN 9780811765770 (e-book) | ISBN
    9780811716222 (paperback : alk. paper)
Subjects: LCSH: Knitting—Patterns. | Clothing and dress.
Classification: LCC TT825 (ebook) | LCC TT825 .K635 2017 (print) | DDC 746.43/2—dc23
LC record available at https://lccn.loc.gov/2017018882

First Edition

Printed in the United States of America

♾™ The paper used in this publication meets the minimum requirements of American National Standard for
Information Sciences—Permanence of Paper for Printed Library Materials, ANSI/NISO Z39.48-1992.

Contents

Introduction

Most knitters I know always have a few projects on the needles at any given time, I believe not out of a lack of attention span but because there are a variety of knitting cravings to satisfy. Just as we sometimes hunger for savory or hearty items and sometimes for sweet treats, our knitting palates are wide-ranging. I think of intricate lace shawls and Fair Isle or cabled sweaters—larger projects that take concentration and a little patience—as "savory." On the other hand, quick-to-knit colorful cowls, scarves, fingerless mitts, hats, and the like are decidedly "sweet," and this book is filled with such delectable morsels. Sure, you'll find cables, bobbles, texture, lace, and colorwork, but all in bite-size pieces that make them deliciously indulgent.

Each project can easily be cast on and bound off in just a few hours. Of course, knitting speed varies widely, but we asked our designers to focus on projects that could be completed in three hours or less by the average knitter. Some may take slightly more time and others quite a bit less. But with the knowledge that the time commitment is small and the possibly new skill elements worked over a small span of knitting, I hope that you'll be encouraged to try color-work or cables, bobbles or lace, or other techniques that you might find intimidating on a larger item. At the end of the day, you'll have a gorgeous new piece of knitwear or a fabulous hand-knit gift.

Great for stash-busting or using small amounts of a luxury yarn, the patterns in this book will satisfy your "candy knitting" cravings every time!

Candi Derr

ZIGZAG HEADBAND

Design by Sarah Sundermeyer

This unique headband is perfect for keeping your ears warm on cold winter mornings. Knit with just a quarter of a skein of worsted weight yarn, it can be whipped up in an hour or two. Increases and decreases are used throughout the headband to create its interesting zigzag shape, and a simple lace pattern adds interest and texture. It is knit end to end, and the headband tapers off into points to allow for a simple button closure at the back of the neck.

FINISHED MEASUREMENTS

22 x 2 in. (56 x 5 cm)

YARN

Malabrigo Rios; medium weight #4 yarn; 100% merino wool; 210 yd. (192 m) and 3.5 oz. (100 g) per skein
» 1 skein #136 Sabiduria *Project usage: 45–60 yd. (41–55 m)*

NEEDLES AND OTHER MATERIALS

» U.S. size 6 (4 mm) knitting needles
» Stitch marker
» Small button

GAUGE

20 sts x 24 rows in St st, blocked = 4 in. (10 cm)
Adjust needle size if necessary to obtain gauge.

STITCH PATTERN

Zigzag Stitch
Rows 1, 3, 5, and 7: K2, yo, k2tog, ssk, [k2, yo] twice, k2tog, k1.
Rows 2, 4, 6, and 8: P2, yo, p2tog, p6, yo, p2tog, p1.
Rows 9, 11, 13, and 15: K2, yo, k2tog, k1, yo, k2, k2tog, k1, yo, k2tog, k1.
Rows 10, 12, 14, and 16: P2, yo, p2tog, p6, yo, p2tog, p1.

Headband

CO 4 sts.

Increases

Rows 1, 3, and 5: Purl.
Row 2: K2, yo, k2.
Row 4: K1, kfb, kfb, k2.
Row 6: K2, yo, k3, yo, k2.
Row 7: P2, yo, p2tog, p2, yo, p2tog, p1.
Row 8: K2, yo, k2, yo, k3, yo, k2.
Row 9: P2, yo, p2tog, p5, yo, p2tog, p1.

Row 10: K2, yo, k2tog, k1, yo, k4, yo, k2tog, k1.
Rows 11 and 13: P2, yo, p2tog, p6, yo, p2tog, p1.
Rows 12 and 14: K2, yo, k2tog, k1, yo, k2, k2tog, k1, yo, k2tog, k1.
Row 15: P2, yo, p2tog, p6, yo, p2tog, p1.

Chart

Work the stitch pattern from Zigzag Chart (page 5) or written instructions (page 3) 7 times.
Work Rows 1–12 of the stitch pattern once more, then begin decreasing.

Decreases

Row 1: K2, yo, k2tog, k1, yo, k1, k2tog, k2tog, yo, k2tog, k1.

Row 2: P2, yo, p2tog, p5, yo, p2tog, p1.

Row 3: K2, yo, k3tog, yo, k2tog, k2tog, yo, k2tog, k1.

Row 4: P2, yo, p2tog, p3, yo, p2tog, p1.

Row 5: K2, yo, k2tog, k3tog, yo, k2tog, k1.

Row 6: P2, yo, p2tog, p1, yo, p2tog, p1.

Row 7: K2, yo, k3tog, yo, k2tog, k1.

Row 8: P2, yo, p2tog, yo, p2tog, p1.

Row 9: K2, k2tog, k2tog, k1.

Row 10: P2, p2tog, p1.

BO all sts knitwise.

Finishing

Block out the zigzag edges and sew a button that will fit through the yarn over on Row 2 onto the BO end of the headband.

Zigzag Chart

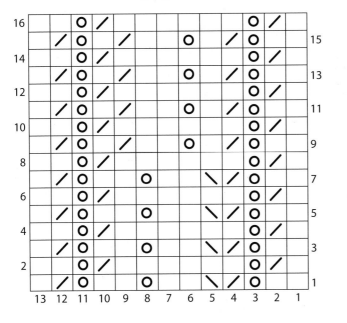

About Sarah Sundermeyer

Sarah loves designing quick, useful knits for any season, and specializes in accessories with rich textures and elegant shapes. She is constantly working on new patterns, inspired by her prodigious yarn stash and the world around her. She has been knitting for many years, and continues to develop her skills in knitting, designing, spinning, dyeing, and crocheting.

HOMAGE TO MRS. HUNTER COWL

Design by Neisha Abdulla

*H*omage to Mrs. Hunter Cowl is a practical and versatile knit that will add to any wardrobe. The piece can be worn as a cozy neck warmer or a stylish headband.

FINISHED MEASUREMENTS

Circumference: Approximately 20 in. (51 cm)
Depth: Approximately 5 in. (13 cm)

YARN

Debbie Bliss Winter Garden; super bulky #6 yarn; 30% llama, 30% wool, 20% silk, 20% linen; 109 yd. (100 m) and 3.5 oz. (100 g) per hank
  » 1 hank #02 Autumn Leaf

NEEDLES AND OTHER MATERIALS

  » U.S. size 13 (9 mm) 16 in. (40 cm) circular needle or a set of 5 double-pointed needles
  » Stitch marker
  » Tapestry needle

GAUGE

10 sts x 16 rows = 4 in. (10 cm)
Adjust needle size if necessary to obtain gauge.

Pattern

CO 52 sts and join to work in the round, being careful to make sure sts are not twisted. Place marker for beginning of round.

Rnd 1: Knit.

Rnd 2: *Sl 1, k3, psso; rep from * to end of rnd.

Rnd 3: *K3, yo; rep from * to end of rnd.

Rnd 4: Knit.

Rnd 5: Knit.

Rnd 6: *Sl 1, k3, psso; rep from * to end of rnd.

Rnd 7: *K3, yo; rep from * to end of rnd.

Rep Rnds 4–7 three times more.

BO all sts. *Note:* Since you will be binding off yarn overs, the last st will require a little neatening up with a tapestry needle.

About Neisha Abdulla

Neisha Abdullah lives in Ireland with her rescue pets, Dotty and Lal. She holds a degree in Art and Design and enjoys creating with many different mediums—yarn and fabric included.

TWIZZLE MITTS AND HAT

Design by Claire Slade

These simple, unisex mitts have a hidden secret: They are completely reversible! The swirling texture of the mitts is further enhanced by the wonderful striping Noro Kureyon yarn. The Twizzle Hat is the perfect accompaniment to the Twizzle Mitts, with the textured welts twirling all the way from the ribbing to the crown. This hat is extremely stretchy and will fit most adult heads.

TWIZZLE MITTS

FINISHED MEASUREMENTS

Very stretchy, to fit adult hand 6–9 in.
    (15–23 cm) around knuckle
Actual measurements: 7.5 in. (19 cm) circum-
    ference x 7 in. (17.75 cm) length

YARN

Noro Kureyon; medium weight #4 yarn;
100% wool; 110 yd. (100.5 m) and 1.7 oz.
(50 g) per skein
    » 1 skein #301 *Project usage: approximately
    100 yd. (91 m)*

NEEDLES AND OTHER MATERIALS

    » U.S. size 7 (4.5 mm) double-pointed
    needles

GAUGE

18 sts in pattern = 4 in. (10 cm)
Adjust needle size if necessary to obtain gauge.

Mitt (Make 2)

Cuff

CO 32 sts and join to work in the round being
  careful not to twist.

Rnd 1: *K2, p2; rep from * to end of round.
Rnd 2: P1, *k2, p2; rep from * to last 3 sts, k2, p1.
Rnd 3: *P2, k2; rep from * to end of round.
Rnd 4: K1, *p2, k2; rep from * to last 3 sts, p2, k1.
Repeat Rnds 1–4 until work measures 4 in. (10
  cm), ending with Rnd 4.

Thumb Opening

Note: This section of the mitt is worked flat back
  and forth in rows.

Row 1 (RS): *K2, p2; rep from * to end, turn.
Row 2 (WS): K1, *p2, k2; rep from * to last 3 sts,
  p2, k1, turn.
Row 3: *P2, k2; rep from * to end, turn.

Row 4: P1, *k2, p2; rep from * to last 3 sts, k2, p1,
  turn.
Repeat these 4 rows until thumb opening measures 2 in. (5 cm), ending with Row 4.

Hand

Ensuring that the RS of the work is facing you,
  rejoin to work in the round and repeat the
  original Rnds 1–4 until the mitt measures 7 in.
  (17.75 cm).
Loosely BO all sts in pattern.

Finishing

Block the mitt gently and weave in ends.
If you want the swirls on each mitt to go in
  opposite directions then just turn one mitt
  inside out.

TWIZZLE HAT

FINISHED MEASUREMENTS

To fit adult head 20–23 in. (51–58 cm)
  circumference
Actual measurement: 21½ in. (54.5 cm)
  circumference, unstretched

YARN

Noro Kureyon; medium weight #4 yarn;
100% wool; 110 yd. (100.5 m) and 1.7 oz.
(50 g) per skein
  » 2 skeins #301 *Project usage:*
    approximately 130 yd. (119 m)

NEEDLES AND OTHER MATERIALS

  » U.S. size 6 (4 mm) 16 in. (40 cm)
    circular needle
  » U.S. size 7 (4.5 mm) 16 in. (40 cm)
    circular needle
  » U.S. size 7 (4.5 mm) double-pointed
    needles

GAUGE

18 sts in pattern = 4 in. (10 cm)
Adjust needle size if necessary to obtain gauge.

Hat

Ribbing

Using the smaller needles, CO 96 sts and join to work in the round being careful not to twist.

Ribbing rnd: *K2, p2; rep from * to end of round.

Repeat ribbing rnd until work measures 1 in. (2.5 cm).

Body of Hat

Change to larger needles.

Rnd 1: *K2, p2; rep from * to end of round.

Rnd 2: P1, *k2, p2; rep from * to last 3 sts, k2, p1.

Rnd 3: *P2, k2; rep from * to end of round.

Rnd 4: K1, *p2, k2; rep from * to last 3 sts, p2, k1.

Repeat Rnds 1–4 until hat measures 6 in. (15.25 cm), ending with Rnd 4.

Crown Decreases

Note: Change to dpns when necessary.

Rnd 1: *[K2, p2] twice, k2, p2tog; rep from * to end of round—88 sts.

Rnd 2: *P1, [k2, p2] twice, k2tog; rep from * to end of round—80 sts.

Rnd 3: *[P2, k2] twice, p2tog; rep from * to end of round—72 sts.

Rnd 4: *K1, p2, k2, p2, k2tog; rep from * to end of round—64 sts.

Rnd 5: *K2, p2, k2, p2tog; rep from * to end of round—56 sts.

Rnd 6: *P1, k2, p2, k2tog; rep from * to end of round—48 sts.

Rnd 7: *P2, k2, p2tog; rep from * to end of round—40 sts.

Rnd 8: *K1, p2, k2tog; rep from * to end of round—32 sts.

Rnd 9: *K2, p2tog; rep from * to end of round—24 sts.

Rnd 10: *P1, k2tog; rep from * to end of round—16 sts.

Rnd 11: *P2tog; rep from * to end of round—8 sts.

Break yarn, thread through the remaining 8 sts, pull tight, and secure.

Finishing

Block the hat lightly and weave in all ends.

About Claire Slade

Claire Slade loves bright, quirky designs with an emphasis on color and/or texture. She has self-published a variety of patterns for unique, colorful hats, shawls, ornaments, and baby clothes, and a full collection of boot cuffs, *A Cocktail Cabinet of Boot Toppers.*

LANCASTER CUFF

Design by Brenda Castiel

*L*ancaster uses a color-changing yarn like Noro to create chevron stripes. The cuff closes with snap fasteners over which decorative buttons are sewn. Choose great vintage buttons for a funky or steampunk look.

FINISHED MEASUREMENTS

Approximately 4 in. (10 cm) x 8$\frac{1}{2}$ in. (21.5 cm)

YARN

Noro Kureyon; medium weight #4 yarn; 100% wool; 110 yd. (101 m) and 1.7 oz. (50 g) per skein
  » 1 skein #052 *Project usage: approximately 37 yd. (34 m)*

NEEDLES AND OTHER MATERIALS

  » U.S. size 7 (4.5 mm) knitting needles
  » 2 buttons
  » 2 snap fasteners
  » Tapestry needle
  » Sewing needle for attaching buttons

GAUGE

16 sts x 20 rows in St st = 4 in. (10 cm)
Adjust needle size if necessary to obtain gauge.

STITCH PATTERN

Chevron Stitch (Multiple of 10 sts)
Row 1: *K2tog, k2, kfb twice, k2, ssk; rep from * to end.
Row 2: Purl.

Cuff

CO 38 sts.

Rows 1–2: Knit.

Row 3 (RS): Sl 1 knitwise, p1, work Row 1 of Chevron Stitch to last 6 sts, [p1, k1] 3 times.

Row 4: Sl 1 purlwise, [k1, p1] twice, k1, purl to last 2 sts, k1, p1.

Rep Rows 3–4 until piece measures 1 in. (2.5 cm).

Rep Row 3.

Knit 1 row.

Rep Rows 3–4 for an additional 1 in. (2.5 cm).

Rep Row 3.

Knit 1 row.

Rep Rows 3–4 for $^3/_4$ in. (2 cm) more.

Knit 2 rows.

BO all sts.

Finishing

Weave in all loose ends, block piece, sew on snap fasteners at desired position.

Sew on buttons over snaps.

About Brenda Castiel

Brenda Castiel has been knitting on and off since she was in her teens, but became somewhat obsessed with it in 2007. Knitting provides a great creative counterpoint to her IT consulting work. She loves squishy wools for the short, mild Los Angeles winters, and likes cottons and blends for the rest of the year. Brenda firmly believes that even beginner knitters can create something beautiful and useful, so she strives to keep patterns simple yet original.

She has had designs published in *Interweave Knits, Creative Knitting, Vogue Knitting, Classic Elite Yarns, KnitPicks,* and *Knit Now.*

GO FOR IT HAT

Design by Christen Comer

*T*his hat is worked in a combination of knits and purls in a bulky weight yarn that, when complete, looks like opposing lines running in opposite directions. This effect occurs whether you use one color or two.

SIZES

Note: Choose size based on head height. The circumference will be determined by how many rows you knit.
Child (Adult Medium, Adult Large)
7 (10, 12) in./18 (25.5, 30.5) cm high

YARN

Lion Brand Wool-Ease Thick & Quick; super bulky #6 yarn; 80% acrylic, 20% wool; 106 yd. (97 m) and 6 oz. (170 g) per skein
» 1 skein for a solid color hat
» 1 skein each for two-color version, any colors (samples shown in #110 Navy/#99 Fisherman and #135 Spice/#189 Butterscotch)

NEEDLES AND OTHER MATERIALS

» U.S. size 13 (9 mm) knitting needles
» Tapestry needle

GAUGE

9 sts x 12 rows = 4 in. (10 cm)
Gauge is not critical for this project. Because you work the hat sideways, you will simply knit until it is the desired circumference and then bind off.

Hat

With Color A, CO 15 (21, 27) sts. Switch to Color B.

Row 1: *K3, p3; rep from * to last 3 sts, k3.

Row 2: *K3, p3; rep from * to last 3 sts, k3.

Switch to Color A.

Rows 3 and 4: Rep Rows 1–2.

Switch to Color B.

Rows 5 and 6: Rep Rows 1–2.

Repeat Rows 3–6, ending with Color B, until piece measures head circumference: Child: 17 in. (43 cm); Adult Medium: 20 in. (51 cm); Adult Large: 22 in. (56 cm).

BO loosely with Color A, leaving a tail approximately 24 in. (61 cm) long. Cut B.

With tapestry needle and A, seam short ends together. Do not cut yarn.

Continuing at top, weave tapestry needle through the topmost loop of row edges, around entire top. Pull tight to create hat. Fasten securely by sewing top closed with tail.

Weave in ends. Block lightly.

About Christen Comer

Christen Comer sells custom hand knits, teaches knitting, repairs knits, finishes knits from seaming to finishing touches, provides sample knitting and technical editing to pattern designs, and more, through her business Christen Knits. Find Christen's novel, *Knitwitch*, on Amazon, available in both paperback and Kindle editions.

ADD A BOW

Design by Faye Kennington

Why buy hair elastics when your rubber stationery supplies can be recycled into adorable scrunchies with bows? Use a longer rubber band for a headband. Either way, it's a quick and fun project using less than .5 oz. (11 g) of scrap yarn.

FINISHED MEASUREMENTS

Scrunchie (Headband)
Circumference: 6–16 (15–40) in./13–24
   (33–71) cm

YARN

KnitPicks Swish DK, light weight #3 yarn;
100% superwash merino wool; 123 yd.
(112.5 m) and 1.7 oz. (50 g) per skein
» 1 skein any color *Project usage:
   approximately 20 (27) yd./18 (25) m*

NEEDLES AND OTHER MATERIALS

» Two U.S. size 4 (3.5 mm) short double-
   pointed needles
» Cable needle
» Tapestry needle
» Thin 3 in. (7 cm) or 6 in. (15 cm) rubber
   band(s), matching the color of the yarn
   if desired

GAUGE

20 sts x 32 rows in St st= 4 in. (10 cm)
Adjust needle size if necessary to obtain gauge.

Pattern

Band

Measure 7 (15) yd./7 (14) m yarn and wind into a small, tight ball. Begin making an I-cord over the rubber band as follows.

CO 3 sts and hold perpendicular across one or two thin 3 in. (7 cm) or 6 in. (15 cm) rubber bands.

Pass yarn ball through rubber band(s) and knit the 3 sts on the dpn. Slide sts to the right end of needle. Pull the yarn snug on the first st to prevent excessive laddering.

Again, pass yarn ball through rubber band(s) and knit the 3 sts on the dpn. Repeat until the rubber band is almost covered. *Note:* Some laddering will occur on the underside; this will lay flat on head or hair without pulling.

Stretch the rubber band out of the ring of knit sts and add on as many more rows of I-cord as you want. The number of knit rows will ultimately dictate how wide the rubber band can be stretched. A scrunchie should be able to stretch up to 8 in. (20 cm) long, and a headband should be able to stretch up to 13 in. (33 cm).

BO all sts and cut the yarn, leaving an 8 in. (20 cm) tail.

Use the tail to sew BO edge to CO edge, making sure I-cord is not twisted.

Bow

Increase

CO 6 sts.

Row 1 (WS): Purl.

Row 2 (RS): K1, M1, knit to last st, M1, k1.
Work previous 2 rows 3 more times—14 sts.
Work 15 rows St st, ending on a WS row.

Cable

Cable Row (RS): Transfer next 5 sts to cn and
   hold to back, wyif of sts on cn knit next 4 sts
   from main needle, k5 sts from cn, transfer rem
   5 sts to cn.
Cable Row (WS): P9 sts from main needle, holding cn to front p5 sts starting with edgemost st.
   Note: Work will appear twisted at this stage.
Work 13 rows St st, ending on RS row.

Decrease

Row 1 (WS): P1, p2tog, purl to last 3 sts, p2tog,
   p1.
Row 2 (RS): Knit.
Work previous 2 rows 3 more times—6 sts.
BO and cut yarn, leaving an 8 in. (20 cm) tail.

Use tail yarn to whipstitch bow CO edge to BO
   edge. Tack this seam to the underside of the
   bow's cable.

Finishing

Sew the bow onto the band over top of the join
   seam. Take care not to stitch through rubber
   band. Secure and sew in loose ends.

About Faye Kennington

Faye Kennington makes her life on the remote western edge of Vancouver Island in a place known to locals as "Ukee." Stormy winters make an excellent excuse for throwing some logs on the wood stove and swatching away. Owning and operating a small tourism business in the summer months proves a fulfilling distraction when the weather is nice.

A zillion years ago, she attended fashion design school and during her early years, she aspired to design shoes. However, most of her career positions were dedicated to Human Resource Management. This combined interest in design and Excel spreadsheet know-how have made a good basis for knitwear design.

CHESHIRE CAT COWL

Design by Kristen Polotsky

This cowl was inspired by classic, muted fashions of the past, but with a modern spin. The color and button are vintage-looking but the overall stitch design is modern. This cowl is versatile enough to go with a simple dress or a long-sleeve T-shirt and jeans. The bulky yarn, large needles, and spaces left from the yarn overs make this a very quick knit.

FINISHED MEASUREMENTS

5³/₄ in. (14.5 cm) x 29 in. (73.5 cm)

YARN

Manos del Uruguay Wool Clasica; medium weight #4 yarn; 100% wool; 138 yd. (126 m) and 3.5 oz. (100 g) per skein
» 1 skein #52 Cameo

NEEDLES AND OTHER MATERIALS

» U.S. size 15 (10 mm) knitting needles
» 1³/₄ in. (4.5 cm) diameter button

GAUGE

11 sts x 6 rows in pattern = 4 in. (10 cm)
Adjust needle size if necessary to obtain gauge.

Cowl

CO 16 sts.

Rows 1–2: Knit.

Row 3: K6, yo, k1, yo twice, k1, yo three times, k1, yo twice, k1, yo, k6.

Row 4: Knit, dropping all yarn overs off the needle.

Rows 5–6: Knit.

Row 7: K1, yo, k1, yo twice, k1, yo three times, k1, yo twice, k1, yo, k6, yo, k1, yo twice, k1, yo three times, k1, yo twice, k1, yo, k6.

Row 8: Knit, dropping all yarn overs off the needle.

Rep Rows 1–8 until piece measures approximately 29 in. (73.5 cm) from beginning.

BO.

Finishing

Weave in ends and block.

Sew button onto a center garter section about 6 in. (15.25 cm) away from the BO edge. Use one of the spaces in the "Cheshire cat" stitch pattern on the opposite end as a buttonhole. Try different spaces for different looks.

About Kristen Polotsky

Residing in Chicago, Kristen Polotsky especially loves knitting scarves and shawls, but creates just about anything that can be made with needles and yarn.

ONE-ROW TRIPLE-WRAP BRACELET

Design by Ellen Harvey

*S*pend an hour making this bracelet and you will be hooked on knitting with beads. You will find the supplies in most craft stores. Look for Japanese beads, as they have larger center holes, making them easier to thread onto your yarn. The bracelet can also be worn as a necklace.

FINISHED MEASUREMENTS

20 in. (51 cm) long

YARN

DMC Perle Cotton; 100% cotton; 27 yd. (25 m) per skein
  » 1 skein #801 (brown) or #400 (rust)

NEEDLES AND OTHER MATERIALS

  » U.S. size 2 (2.75 mm) knitting needles
  » 118 size 6 glass beads
  » Large eye beading needle or dental floss threader
  » Tapestry needle
  » 1/4 in. (8 mm) button clasp
  » Coordinating sewing thread
  » Sewing needle

GAUGE

6 sts = 1 in. (2.5 cm)
Adjust needle size if necessary to obtain gauge.

NOTES

  » Treat the perle cotton just like a skein of yarn: Open it up and wind into a ball before using it.
  » The beads are threaded on before the cast-on.
  » Every stitch except the first and last have a bead knitted into them.

STITCH GUIDE

PB & K means to place a bead in each knit stitch. Simply insert your working needle into the stitch, slide a bead down to the needle, and complete the knit stitch.

Bracelet

Using the beading needle or floss threader, slide 118 beads onto the perle cotton. Push them down to free up a length of yarn to cast on. CO 120 sts.

Row 1: K1, *PB & K; rep from * to last st, k1. BO all sts.

Finishing

Use the sewing needle and thread to sew the button clasp components, one on each end. Use the tapestry needle to weave in the CO and BO ends.

About Ellen Harvey

Ellen Harvey is a lifelong knitter, Master Level 1 knitter by The Knitting Guild of America, and Certified Instructor by the Craft Yarn Council of America. She teaches knitting in various settings in New York and Connecticut. Her patterns have been published in several books, including *One-Skein Wonders for Babies*, *Lace One-Skein Wonders*, *Page-a-Day Pattern Calendars*, and *Simple Knits for Sophisticated Living*.

CABLED BEANIE

Design by Szilvia Linczmaier

This cabled hat features unusually huge 3D-like cables that are unique and stylish. This feminine hat is seamless and perfect for chilly winter days.

FINISHED MEASUREMENTS

One size fits most adults.
Head circumference: 20–22 in. (51–56 cm)
Width (relaxed at widest point): 9 in. (22 cm)
Brim length: 1³/₄ in. (4.5 cm)
Full length: 9 in. (22 cm)

YARN

Malabrigo Mecha; bulky weight #5 yarn;
100% merino wool; 130 yd. (119 m) and
3.5 oz. (100 g) per skein
  » 2 skeins #033 Cereza (red) or #051 VAA
    (teal) *Project usage: approximately 157 yd.
    (143.5 m)*

NEEDLES AND OTHER MATERIALS

  » U.S. size 7 (4.5 mm) double-pointed
    needles
  » U.S. size 7 (4.5 mm) 16 in. (40 cm)
    circular needle
  » U.S. size 10¹/₂ (6.5 mm) double-pointed
    needles
  » U.S. size 10¹/₂ (6.5 mm) 16 in. (40 cm)
    circular needle
  » U.S. size 6 (4 mm) double-pointed
    needles or circular needle (optional: see
    Notes)
  » Stitch marker
  » Cable needle
  » Tapestry needle

GAUGE

13 sts x 20 rows in St st with larger needles, after blocking = 4 in. (10 cm)
Adjust needle size if necessary to obtain gauge.
Note: The measurements of the sample knit in Malabrigo Mecha remained the same after blocking.

NOTES

» The hat is knitted seamlessly from the bottom up.
» Use U.S. size 6 (4 mm) needles for the brim if you want a circumference on the smaller side, 20–21 in. (51–53 cm).
» For a video of long-tail cast-on over two needles, visit youtube.com/watch?v =lrW2IKWemmY.
» For a video on how to Make 1 (M1), visit youtube.com/watch?v=f7o ABJLKZtw.

Beanie

CO 84 sts with U.S. 6 (4 mm) or 7 (4.5 mm) needles, depending on size desired (see Notes), using long-tail cast-on over two needles or your preferred cast-on.
Join in the round, be careful not to twist stitches. Place marker at beginning of round.

Brim
Rnds 1–11: *K1, p1; rep from * to end of round.

Body
Rnd 1 (inc): *K3, M1; rep from * to end of round—112 sts.
Change to size 10½ (6.5 mm) needles.
Rnds 2–6: Knit.
Rnd 7: *Put 4 sts on cn and move to back of work, k4, k4 from cn, put 4 sts on cn and move to front of work, k4, k4 from cn; rep from * to end of round.

Rnds 8–23 (16 rnds): Knit.
Rnd 24: Knit to end of round, remove marker, k4, place marker (this will be your new beg of round marker).

Crown
Rnd 1: *K8, put 4 sts on cn and move to back of work, k4, k4 from cn; rep from * to end of round.
Rnds 2–3: Knit.
Rnd 4: Rep Rnd 1.
Rnd 5: Knit.
Rnd 6: Knit to end of round, remove marker, k4, place marker (this will be your new beg of round marker).
Rnd 7: *K8, put 4 sts on cn and move to front of work, k2, ssk, [k2tog, k2] from cn; rep from * to end of round—98 sts.
Rnds 8–9: Knit.
Rnd 10: *Put 4 sts on cn and move to front of work, k2, ssk, [k2tog, k2] from cn, k6; rep from * to end of round—84 sts.
Rnd 11: Knit.
Rnd 12: *Put 6 sts on cn and move to back of work, k2, [k2tog] twice, [k2tog twice, k2] from cn; rep from * to end of round—56 sts.
Rnd 13: Knit.
Rnd 14: *K2tog, ssk, [k2tog] twice; rep from * to end of round—28 sts.
Rnd 15: Knit.
Rnd 16: *K2tog, ssk; rep from * to end of round—14 sts.
Rnd 17: *Ssk; rep from * to end of round—7 sts.

Finishing

Break yarn, leaving a 6 in. (15 cm) tail. Using a tapestry needle, pull the tail through the last 7 sts and pull tight to close top of hat. Weave in all ends. Block as desired.

About Szilvia Linczmaier

Szilvia is a mother of three precious girls who has changed her career in finance to designing handmade knitwear. Her field of expertise is feminine accessories. Her designs are elegant but playful, easy to make, and highly wearable. She is regularly inspired by her children.

FAMILY HAT

Design by Szilvia Linczmaier

This is a perfect hat for the whole family. Beanie or slouchy? Make your choice, and you will have a hat that is exactly what you wished for. The sunburst texture at the top will keep you on your toes.

FINISHED MEASUREMENTS

XS: Baby 6–12 Months (S: Toddler, M: Child, L: Teen/Small Adult, XL: Adult, XXL: Large Adult)

Head circumference: 16–17 (17–19, $18^1/_2$–20, $19^1/_2$–$21^1/_2$, 21–23, 22–24) in./40–43 (43–48, 47–51, 49.5–54.5, 53.5–58.5, 56–61) cm

YARN

Malabrigo Rios; medium weight #4 yarn; 100% superwash merino wool; 210 yd. (192 m) and 3.5 oz. (100 g) per skein
» 1 skein #063 Natural *Project usage: 150 yd. (137 m) or less*

NEEDLES AND OTHER MATERIALS

» U.S. size 4 (3.5 mm) double-pointed needles
» U.S. size 7 (4.5 mm) double-pointed needles
» Stitch marker
» Tapestry needle

GAUGE

21 sts x 28 rows in St st with larger needles = 4 in. (10 cm)
Adjust needle size if necessary to obtain gauge.

NOTES

» For a slouchy hat for sizes XS through L, just size up! The brim is stretchy enough to fit a variety of head circumferences. If your head is already a size XL or XXL, follow the slouchy pattern on page 37 for your size.
» The pattern is written for a solid colorway, but you can personalize your hat by using different colorways for the brim and the rest of the hat or by combining several colors at the brim.
» Every size of this hat will fit a wide range of heads, styling loosely on small heads with a folded brim or more tightly on larger heads. Knit a bunch in the same or varying sizes and any member of the family can grab one on their way out the door.

STITCH PATTERN

Seed Stitch
Rnd 1: *K1, p1; rep from * to end of rnd.
Rnd 2: *P1, k1; rep from * to end of rnd.
Repeat Rnds 1–2.

Family Hat

Brim

With smaller needles, CO 72 (78, 84, 88, 94, 100) sts.

Join in the round, being careful not to twist sts. Place marker for beginning of rnd.

Rnd 1: Purl.

Rnds 2–9: Work in Seed Stitch pattern.

Sizes M (L, XL, XXL) only: Work an additional 2 (4, 4, 6) rnds of Seed Stitch pattern, then continue with Rnd 10.

Rnd 10: Purl.

Change to larger needles.

Knit in St stitch (knit every rnd) for 3 (3^1/$_2$, 4, 4^1/$_2$, 5, 5^1/$_4$) in./8 (9, 10, 11.5, 12.5, 13) cm.

Crown

Rnd 1: *K1, sl 1 wyib; rep from * to end of rnd.

Rnd 2: *P1, k1; rep from * to end of rnd.

Rnd 3: Rep Rnd 1.

Rnd 4: Knit.

Rnd 5: *K2tog; rep from * to end of rnd—36 (39, 42, 44, 47, 50) sts.

Sizes XS (M, L, XXL) only:

Rnd 6: *P1, k1; rep from * to end of rnd.

Rnd 7: *K1, sl 1 wyib; rep from * to end of rnd.

Size S (XL) only:

Rnd 6: *P1, k1; rep from * until 1 st remains, p1.

Rnd 7: *K1, sl 1 wyib; rep from * until 1 st remains, k1.

All Sizes:

Rnd 8: Knit.

Sizes XS (M, L, XXL) only:

Rnd 9: *K2tog; rep from * to end of rnd—18 (21, 22, 25) sts.

Sizes S (XL) only:

Rnd 9: *K2tog; rep from * until 1 st remains, k1—20 (24) sts.

Sizes XS (S, L, XL) only:

Rnd 10: *P1, k1; rep from * to end of rnd.

Rnd 11: *K1, sl 1 wyib; rep from * to end of rnd.

Sizes M (XXL) only:

Rnd 10: *P1, k1; rep from * until 1 st remains, p1.

Rnd 11: *K1, sl 1 wyib; rep from * until 1 st remains, k1.

All Sizes:

Rnd 12: Knit.

Sizes XS (S, L, XL) only:

Rnd 13: *K2tog; rep from * to end of rnd.

Sizes M (XXL) only:

Rnd 13: *K2tog; rep from * until 1 st remains, k1.

At the end of Rnd 13, 9 (10, 11, 11, 12, 13) sts remain.

Finishing

Cut yarn, leaving a tail approximately 8 in. (20 cm) long. Thread tail through remaining sts with a tapestry needle and pull tight to close the hole. Weave in all ends. No blocking required!

Slouchy Version for Sizes XL and XXL

Sizes are set up as follows: XL (XXL).

Brim

With smaller needles, CO 94 (100) sts.

Join in the round, being careful not to twist sts. Place marker for beg of rnd.

Rnd 1: Purl.

Rnds 2–13: Work in Seed Stitch pattern.

Size XXL only: Work an additional two rnds in Seed Stitch pattern, then continue with Rnd 14.

Rnd 14: Purl all stitches, increasing 6 (4) sts evenly—100 (104) sts.

Change to larger needles.

Knit in St st (knit every rnd) for 6 (6.5) in./15 (16) cm or for desired length.

Crown

Rnd 1: *K1, sl 1 wyib; rep from * to end of rnd.

Rnd 2: *P1, k1; rep from * to end of rnd.

Rnd 3: Rep Rnd 1.

Rnd 4: Knit.

Rnd 5: *K2tog; rep from * to end of rnd—50 (52) sts.

Rnd 6: *P1, k1; rep from * to end of rnd.

Rnd 7: *K1, sl 1 wyib; rep from * to end of rnd.

Rnd 8: Knit.

Rnd 9 : *K2tog; rep from * to end of rnd—25 (26) sts.

Size XL only:

Rnd 10: *P1, k1; rep from * until 1 st remains, p1.

Rnd 11: *K1, sl 1 wyib; rep from * until 1 st remains, k1.

Size XXL only:

Rnd 10: *P1, k1; rep from * to end of rnd.

Rnd 11: *K1, sl 1 wyib; rep from * to end of rnd.

All sizes:

Rnd 12: Knit.

Size XL only:

Rnd 13: *K2tog; rep from * until 1 st remains, k1.

Size XXL only:

Rnd 13: *K2tog; rep from * to end of rnd—13 sts.

Finishing

Cut yarn, leaving a tail approximately 8 in. (20 cm) long. Thread tail through remaining sts with a tapestry needle and pull tight to close the hole. Weave in all ends. No blocking required!

SPRINGSTEP BOOT CUFFS

Design by Michelle May

These fun and flirty boot cuffs are just the thing to brighten up your outfit with no effort at all. The thick wool yarn gives extra warmth for winter, while the airy lace pattern keeps them stylish through to spring. Best of all, you fast knitters will be able to finish a pair of cuffs in just an hour or two!

FINISHED MEASUREMENTS

Circumference: 13–15 in. (33–38 cm)
To adjust the size, see Alternate Sizing sidebar.

YARN

Manos del Uruguay Wool Clasica; medium weight #4 yarn; 100% wool; 138 yd. (126 m) and 3.5 oz. (100 g) per skein
  » 1 skein #705 Copper

NEEDLES AND OTHER MATERIALS

  » U.S. size 7 (4.5 mm) short circular needle or double-pointed needles
  » U.S. size 10 (6 mm) short circular needle or double-pointed needles
  » Stitch marker
  » Tapestry needle

GAUGE

5 sts in 2x2 rib (stretched slightly) on U.S. size 7 (4.5 mm) needles = 1 in. (2.5 cm)
Adjust needle size if necessary to obtain gauge.

ALTERNATE SIZING

The pattern as written will result in a pair of cuffs to fit circumference 13–15 in. (33–38 cm) when knitted with worsted weight yarn to the stated gauge. To substitute a lighter or heavier weight yarn, you'll need to do a bit of very simple math.

1. Measure your leg where you'd like the cuff to sit to get your desired circumference in inches. This number will be **A**.
2. Knit a swatch of 2x2 rib and check your gauge. Your number of stitches per inch will be **B**.
3. Multiply **A** by **B** to get the total number of stitches you need. Round the result up or down to the closest multiple of 12, this is **C** and will be your **cast-on number**.

Example 1: My desired circumference is 14 in. and my gauge is 6 sts per inch. I need 84 stitches. This is already a multiple of 12, so I can cast on and knit at this number for the entire piece.

Example 2: My desired circumference is 14 in. and my gauge is 4.5 sts per inch. I need 63 stitches. My closest multiples of 12 are 60 and 72, which should give me a finished circumference of 13.3 in. and 16 in., respectively. Since ribbing is stretchy and I want my cuffs to be snug, I choose to cast on 60 sts.

Cuff (Make 2)

CO 60 sts or your calculated number (multiple of 12) with smaller needles.

Join to work in the rnd and pm to mark beg of rnd.

Rnd 1: *K2, p2; rep from * to end of rnd.

Repeat previous rnd until ribbing measures 2 in. (5 cm).

Switch to larger needles.

Next rnd: Knit.

Lace Section

Rnd 1: *Sl 1, k2, psso, k3; rep from * to end of rnd.
Rnd 2: *K1, yo, k4; rep from * to end of rnd.
Rnd 3: *K3, sl 1, k2, psso; rep from * to end of rnd.
Rnd 4: *K4, yo, k1; rep from * to end of rnd.

Work Rnds 1–4 four times or until boot cuff measures 1 in. (2.5 cm) less than your desired finished length.

Work Rnd 1 one final time.

Increase rnd: *K5, M1; rep from * to end of rnd.

Switch to smaller needles.

Next rnd: *K2, p2; rep from * to end of rnd.

Repeat previous rnd until ribbing measures 1 in. (2.5 cm).

Bind off with your favorite stretchy bind-off or search online for Jeny's Surprisingly Stretchy Bind-Off.

Finishing

Weave in ends and block.

About Michelle May

Michelle May strives to make her patterns accessible to all knitters, with easy-to-substitute yarn choices and clear instructions.

AMELIA COWL

Design by Neisha Abdulla

The Amelia Cowl is a light and airy accessory that will still add all the warmth you need for your winter ensemble. The stitch is such that the end result is a very stretchy, open fabric with a cloud-like feel that allows the neck to breathe while still retaining heat.

FINISHED MEASUREMENTS

Circumference: Approximately 40 in.
(114 cm), unstretched
Depth: Approximately 6 in. (15 cm), unstretched

YARN

Debbie Bliss Paloma; super bulky #6 yarn;
60% alpaca, 40% wool; 73 yd. (67 m) and
1.7 oz. (50 g) per skein
» 1 skein #007 Rust

NEEDLES AND OTHER MATERIALS

» U.S. size 19 (15 mm) knitting needles
» Tapestry needle

GAUGE

10 sts x 4 rows = 4 in. (10 cm)
*Gauge is not terribly important due to the nature
of the stitch.*

1. Take the yarn around the back of the RH needle as you would to make a knit stitch.

2. Take the yarn around the front of the LH needle.

3. Take the yarn around the back of the RH needle again.

This will be the resulting stitch.

4. Pull the stitch through as you would with a regular knit stitch.

Cowl

Loosely CO 14 sts.

Insert the RH needle into the first st on the LH needle. Take the yarn around the back of the RH needle as if to knit, then between the two needles to the front of the LH needle, then back around the RH needle—finally knitting the stitch in the usual manner. The first two wraps (around the RH then the LH needle) will drop to form a twisted, elongated garter stitch.

Work all sts on all rows in the same manner until 40 rows have been worked.

Graft the ends together using three-needle bind-off or sew together with a tapestry needle.

Finishing

Weave in ends and block.

CABLED COWL, HAT, WRIST WARMERS, AND MITTS

Design by Kath Andrews

This set was inspired by the idea of working in two directions. The cowl and wrist warmers are worked flat and grafted. The sides of these then become the base from which the hat and mitts are worked at right angles. The simple cable design used throughout becomes very dramatic in super chunky yarn and creates a cozy set to keep you warm.

FINISHED MEASUREMENTS

Cowl: $4^1/_2$ in. (11.5 cm) x 19 in. (48.5 cm) circumference

Hat: $8^1/_2$ in. (21.5 cm) x 19 in. (48.5 cm) circumference

Wrist warmers: $4^1/_2$ in. (11.5 cm) x $6^1/_2$ in. (16.5 cm) circumference

Mitts: 8 in (20.5 cm) x $6^1/_2$ in. (16.5 cm) circumference

YARN

Mirasol Ushya, super bulky #6 yarn; 98% wool, 2% polyamide; 115 yd. (105 m) and 3.5 oz. (100 g) per skein
  » 2 skeins Cherry Red *Note:* Every scrap of two skeins is used when making the complete set—you may wish to buy three to be on the safe side.

NEEDLES AND OTHER MATERIALS

  » U.S. size 15 (10 mm) double-pointed needles
  » U.S. size 15 (10 mm) 16 in. (40 cm) circular needle
  » U.S. P-15 (10 mm) crochet hook for provisional cast-on
  » Waste super chunky/bulky yarn for provisional cast-on
  » Large tapestry needle for weaving in ends and grafting

GAUGE

13 sts x 15 rows in main pattern = 4 in. (10 cm)
Adjust needle size if necessary to obtain gauge.

STITCH GUIDE

C6B (cable 6 back): Slip 3 sts onto cable needle and hold to back, k3 from left-hand needle, k3 from cable needle.

COWL

With waste yarn and U.S. 15 (10 mm) crochet
  hook, make a chain at least 14 chains long. With
  U.S. 15 (10 mm) circular needle, pick up 14 sts
  from the back of the provisional crochet chain.
  (If you prefer, you may work the provisional
  chain directly around the knitting needle to save
  picking up the sts from the chain afterward.)
Using main yarn, work set-up row as follows: K1,
  p3, k6, p3, k1.

Cable Pattern
Row 1 (WS): Sl 1 purlwise, k3, p6, k3, p1.
Row 2 (RS): Sl 1 purlwise, p3, C6B, p3, k1.
Row 3: Rep Row 1.
Row 4: Sl 1 purlwise, p3, k6, p3, k1.
Row 5: Rep Row 1.
Row 6: Rep Row 4.*
Repeat the six-row Cable Pattern another 11 times,
  finishing after Row 4 (RS) on the 11th repeat.

Cut yarn, leaving approximately 20 in. (50 cm) for
  grafting.
Remove provisional crochet chain and place sts
  onto another size 15 (10 mm) needle. Using a
  tapestry needle, graft the two ends together,
  maintaining the stitch pattern as set to keep the
  join invisible.

Finishing
Weave yarn ends in on reverse.** Wet block and
  dry flat.

HAT

Work as for Cowl up to **.
Using US 15 (10 mm) needles (dpns or circular),
  with RS facing, pick up and knit 54 sts from the
  row *behind* the slipped stitch edging of one side
  of the knitting. You will be picking up 3 sts from
  every 4 rows. If using a circular needle, change
  to dpns when work becomes too small to fit
  comfortably on circular needle.
Working in the round:
Rnds 1 and 2: Knit.
Rnd 3: [K7, k2tog] 6 times—48 sts.
Rnds 4 and 5: Knit.
Rnd 6: [K6, k2tog] 6 times—42 sts.
Rnds 7 and 8: Knit.
Rnd 9: [K5, k2tog] 6 times—36 sts.
Rnds 10 and 11: Knit.
Rnd 12: [K4, k2tog] 6 times—30 sts.
Rnd 13: Knit.
Rnd 14: [K3, k2tog] 6 times—24 sts.

Rnd 15: Knit.
Rnd 16: [K2, k2tog] 6 times—18 sts.
Rnd 17: Knit.
Rnd 18: [K1, k2tog] 6 times—12 sts.
Rnd 19: Knit.
Rnd 20: [K2tog] 6 times—6 sts.
Cut yarn, leaving approximately 8 in. (20 cm). Using a tapestry needle, thread yarn through remaining 6 sts and pull tight.

Finishing

Weave yarn ends in on reverse. Wet block and dry flat.

WRIST WARMER
(Make 2)

Work as for Cowl up to *.
Repeat the six-row Cable Pattern another three times, finishing after Row 4 (RS) on the third repeat.
Cut yarn, leaving approximately 20 in. (50 cm) for grafting.
Remove provisional crochet chain and place sts onto another U.S. 15 (10 mm) needle. Using a tapestry needle, graft the two ends together, maintaining the stitch pattern as set to keep the join invisible.

Finishing

Weave yarn ends in on reverse.*** Wet block and dry flat.

MITT (Make 2)

Work as for Wrist Warmer up to ***.
Using U.S. 15 (10 mm) dpns, with RS facing, pick up and knit 18 sts from the row *behind* the slipped stitch edging. You will be picking up 3 sts from every 4 rows.
Working in the round:
Rnds 1–4: Knit.

Thumb Opening
Working in rows:
Row 1: Sl 1 purlwise, knit to end. Turn work.
Row 2: Sl 1 knitwise, purl to end.
Rep these two rows twice more.
Returning to working in the round, knit four rnds.
BO knitwise.

Finishing

Weave yarn ends in on reverse. Wet block and dry flat.

Wrist Warmers

Mitts

About Kath Andrews

Kath Andrews teaches music full-time and has also completed a City and Guilds Level 3 qualification in Hand Knit Textiles, which she found absolutely brilliant for developing skills and ideas. She loves lace, cables, and Fair Isle patterns as well as discovering unusual ways to create and structure things and has had designs published in both the United Kingdom and the United States. She muses, "Many people say to me that they wouldn't have the patience to knit, but I truly believe that knitting is what gives me patience and makes me very happy."

HEADBAND WITH A TWIST

Design by Faith Schmidt

Headband with a Twist is a quick and easy project. Four I-cords are knit separately and braided together. The ends of the braid are then sewn together to form the headband. A small rectangle is knit, wrapped around the seam on the headband, and the edges sewn together, covering the seam, and making it smooth and comfortable on the back of the neck.

FINISHED MEASUREMENTS

Teen/average adult head, approximately 20 in. (51 cm) circumference. Adjust by making I-cords longer or shorter.

YARN

Cascade Yarns 220 Superwash, medium weight #4 yarn; 100% superwash wool; 220 yd.(201 m) and 3.5 oz. (100 g) per skein
  » 1 skein #1910 *Project usage: approximately 40–50 yd. (36–46 m)*

NEEDLES AND OTHER MATERIALS

  » Two U.S. size 7 (4.5 mm) double-pointed needles
  » Tapestry needle
  » Safety pin (optional)

GAUGE

Gauge is not critical for this project.

NOTES

  » This pattern is great for using up small amounts of yarn left over from other projects and gives many color options, as it could be made all in one color, or each I-cord could be knitted in a different color.
  » The easiest way to braid is to secure the beginning of the braid to something fixed, so that it won't move, and you can pull it snug. I found that pinning it to a pillow with a safety pin worked well.

STITCH GUIDE

I-cord: Use two dpns. CO the specified number of sts. *Knit the sts, but do not turn your work at the end of the row. Slide the sts to the other end of the same needle, pull the working yarn behind the sts in preparation to knit the first st again. Rep from * until the I-cord is the required length.

Headband

I-Cord (Make 4)

CO 3 sts. Work an I-cord until the cord is 20 in. (51 cm) long. BO.

After all four cords are finished, weave in all of the ends except those on one cord, leaving one tail on each end to secure the cords together.

Braid

Firmly secure one end of the cords together by running the remaining tail through the end of each cord, several times, and pulling tightly.

Lay cords on a flat surface, securing one end to make it easier to braid. Mentally number the cords 1 to 4, from left to right. Repeat the steps below until braid is desired length.

1. Lift 1 **over** 2.
2. Take 4 **under** 3 and **over** 1.

Tighten up the braid after each repeat, and then mentally renumber the cords as before.

When the braid is complete, firmly secure the ends of the cords by running the remaining tail through the end of each cord, several times, pulling tightly. Sew the braid together, end to end, to reduce bulk.

Slider

CO 10 sts. Work in St st until piece measures 3 in. (7.5 cm). BO, leaving a tail to sew up the seam.

Finishing

Wrap the slider around the seam so that the side edges meet, and whipstitch closed. Weave in ends.

About Faith Schmidt

Faith Schmidt designs under the name DistractedKnits for a very good reason. With nine children in the house, there's always something going on! This has led her to design patterns that are interesting to knit, but are also easy to memorize and "read," in case of one of those all-too-frequent interruptions.

ENTWINED LEAVES SCARF

Design by Quenna Lee

Entwined is a rectangular scarf with a botanical motif. The alternating panels of entwined leaves and garter eyelet provide drape and visual interest.

FINISHED MEASUREMENTS

$5^{1}/_{2}$ x $61^{1}/_{2}$ in. (14 x 156 cm)

YARN

Brown Sheep Company Lamb's Pride Bulky; bulky weight #5 yarn; 85% wool, 15% mohair; 125 yd. (114 m) and 4 oz. (113 g) per skein

» 2 skeins M11 White Frost *Project usage: 180 yd. (165 m)*

NEEDLES AND OTHER MATERIALS

» U.S. size 13 (9 mm) knitting needles
» Tapestry needle

GAUGE

2 repeats of Lace Leaf pattern = $5^{1}/_{2}$ x 6 in. (14 x 15 cm)
1 repeat of Garter Eyelet pattern = $5^{1}/_{2}$ x $1^{1}/_{2}$ in. (14 x 4 cm)
Adjust needle size if necessary to obtain gauge.

STITCH PATTERNS

Lace Leaf (15 sts)
Row 1: Sl 1, k7, k3tog, yo, k1,yo, k3.
Row 2 and all even-numbered rows: Sl 1, k2, p9, k3.
Row 3: Sl 1, k5, k3tog, [k1, yo] twice, k4.
Row 5: Sl 1, k3, k3tog, k2, yo, k1, yo, k5.

Row 7: Sl 1, k2, yo, k1, yo, sk2p, k8.
Row 9: Sl 1, k3, [yo, k1] twice, sk2p, k6.
Row 11: Sl 1, k4, yo, k1, yo, k2, sk2p, k4.
Row 12: Sl 1, k2, p9, k3.
Rep Rows 1–12 for pattern.

Garter Eyelet (odd number of sts)
Rows 1–4: Sl 1, knit to end of row.
Row 5: Sl 1, *yo, k2tog; rep from * to end of row.
Rows 6–8: Sl 1, knit to end of row.

Scarf

CO 15 sts loosely. Work in garter st (knit every row) for 6 rows.

Rows 1–24: Work Lace Leaf pattern/chart twice.

Rows 25–32: Work Garter Eyelet pattern.

Rows 33–224: Rep Rows 1–32 six times.

Rows 225–248: Work Lace Leaf pattern/chart twice.

Work garter st (knit every row) for 6 rows. BO loosely in pattern.

Finishing

Weave in ends. Block to measurements.

Lace Leaf Chart

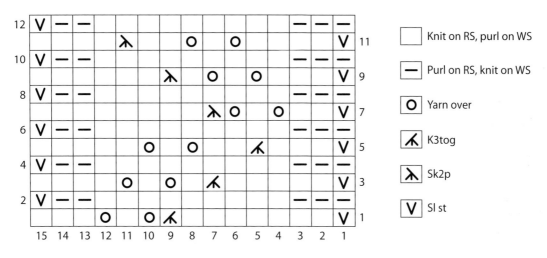

☐	Knit on RS, purl on WS
—	Purl on RS, knit on WS
O	Yarn over
K	K3tog
λ	Sk2p
V	Sl st

Work from the bottom up, right to left. The odd rows are RS and even rows are WS.

About Quenna Lee

Quenna Lee is a prolific designer whose patterns have been published since 2011 in magazines including *Knitscene*, *I Like Knitting*, and *Interweave Knits*, and a variety of publications by Knit Picks, Twist Collective, and Willow Yarns.

GIFT CARD SLEEVE

Design by Dana Gervais

This knitted sleeve is a unique, personalized way to wrap a gift card. It also makes a cute tree ornament. Small and portable, it is ideal for on-the-go knitting and is a great way to use up leftover yarn.

FINISHED MEASUREMENTS

4 in. (10 cm) long x 2^1/$_4$ in. (5.7 cm) wide, after blocking

YARN

Koigu Painter's Palette Premium Merino; super fine #1 weight yarn; 100% merino wool; 175 yd. (160 m) and 1.7 oz. (50 g) per skein

» Approximately ^{1}/$_4$ skein #P453

NEEDLES AND OTHER MATERIALS

» U.S. size 3 (3.25 mm) knitting needles
» Tapestry needle
» Button or ribbon
» 2 stitch holders or 1 spare needle

GAUGE

6 sts in St st, after blocking = 1 in. (2.5 cm)
Gauge is not crucial for this project, however, a different gauge will affect the finished size of the project and the amount of yarn required. Adjust needle size if necessary to obtain gauge.

NOTES

» The envelope flap with buttonhole allows for a decorative button or ribbon closure.
» Clever construction allows you to work this whole piece back and forth in rows with no seaming. This pattern is something like a magic trick; a sleight of hand at the end and a flip inside out, and the piece you knitted in rows is now a sleeve.

Pattern

CO 32 sts.

Row 1: *K1, sl 1; rep from * to end of row.

Rep Row 1 until work measures 3$\frac{1}{2}$ in. (9 cm).

Using spare needles or stitch holders, slip all even sts onto one needle/holder and all odd sts onto another needle/holder.

You now have two needles with 16 sts each.

Turn the gift card sleeve inside out. The stockinette side is on the outside and is now the RS.

BO 16 sts from one needle—16 sts remain on one needle.

Set-up Rows for Envelope Flap

Row 1 (RS): Knit.

Row 2: Purl.

Rep Rows 1–2 twice more.

Envelope Flap

Row 1: K1, ssk, k until last 3 sts, k2tog, k1.

Row 2: Purl all sts.

Repeat Rows 1 and 2 until 6 sts remain.

Row 3: Ssk, k1, yo, k1, k2tog.

Row 4: Purl all sts.

Row 5: Ssk, k1, k2tog.

Row 6: Purl all sts.

Row 7: Sl 1, k2tog, psso.

Cut yarn and secure tail through remaining st.

Finishing

Weave in ends and block.

Add button or ribbon closure to envelope flap.

About Dana Gervais

Dana is a knitwear designer specializing in socks! She creates unique, beautiful knitting patterns that are graded for multiple sizes. She is a sarcastic, nerdy, yarn-loving, obsessive knitter who finds inspiration in anything and everything.

Dana has far more ideas than time and her yarn stash has its own bedroom in her house. Dana lives in Ontario, Canada, with her amazing husband, two super-awesome kids, two furry-lovey dogs, and two fluffy-charming cats.

BOMBER BEANIE

Design by Quenna Lee

omber is a chunky beanie, requiring only one skein. It is worked in the round from the bottom up with a garter rim and a simple fishtail lace pattern.

FINISHED MEASUREMENTS

Height: 8 in. (20.5 cm)
Circumference at brim: 24 in. (61 cm)

YARN

Lion Brand Alpine Wool; bulky weight #5 yarn; 100% wool; 108 yd. (98 m) and 3.5 oz. (100 g) per skein
  » 1 skein #123 Bay Leaf

NEEDLES AND OTHER MATERIALS

  » U.S. size 11 (8 mm) 16 in. (40 cm) circular needle
  » U.S. size 11 (8 mm) double-pointed needles
  » Stitch markers
  » Tapestry needle

GAUGE (IN THE ROUND)

3$\frac{1}{2}$ in. (9 cm) x 1$\frac{3}{4}$ in. (4.5 cm) in Fishtail Lace pattern
12 sts x 20 rnds in garter st = 4 in. (10 cm)
Adjust needle size if necessary to obtain gauge.

STITCH PATTERN

Fishtail Lace (multiple of 12 sts)

Rnd 1: *K5, p7; rep from *.

Rnd 2 and all even-numbered rnds: Knit.

Rnd 3: *K2, yo, k1, yo, k2, p2, p3tog, p2; rep from *.

Rnd 5: *K2, yo, k3, yo, k2, p1, p3tog, p1; rep from *.

Rnd 7: *K2, yo, k5, yo, k2, p3tog; rep from *.

Rnd 8: Knit.

Rep Rnds 1–8 for pattern.

Beanie

Note: To maintain vertical alignment of lace pattern, the beginning of rnd marker needs to move forward as directed below.

CO 72 sts loosely. Place marker and join to work in the rnd, taking care to not twist sts.

Rnd 1: Purl.

Rnds 2–8: Work garter st (alternating knit and purl rows), beginning and ending with a knit row.

Rnds 9–16: Work one rep of Fishtail Lace pattern.

Rnds 17–24: Remove marker, k3, place marker; work one rep of Fishtail Lace pattern.

Decrease

Rnd 25: Remove marker, k3, place marker, work Rnd 1 of Fishtail Lace pattern.

Rnd 26: Knit.

Rnd 27: *K2, yo, k1, yo, k2, p2tog, p3tog, p2tog; rep from *—60 sts.

Rnd 28: Knit.

Rnd 29: *K2, yo, k3, yo, k2, p3tog; rep from *.

Rnd 30: Knit.

Rnd 31: Remove marker, k1, place marker, *k7, sk2p; rep from *—48 sts.

Rnd 32: Remove marker, k1, place marker, *k5, sk2p; rep from *—36 sts.

Rnd 33: Remove marker, k1, place marker, *k3, sk2p; rep from *—24 sts.

Rnd 34: Knit.

Rnd 35: Remove marker, k1, place marker, *k1, sk2p; rep from *—12 sts.

Rnd 36: Knit.

Cut yarn, leaving a 10 in. (25.5 cm) tail. With a tapestry needle, pull through remaining sts.

Finishing

Weave and trim ends. Block lightly.

Fishtail Lace Chart

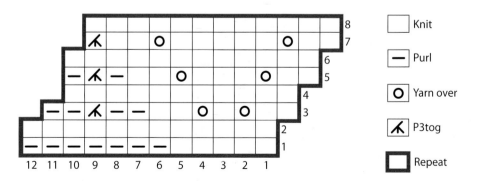

Work from the bottom up, all rounds from right to left.

AUTUMN CHILL LEG WARMERS

Design by Candi Derr

When the weather turns chilly (or downright frosty), these leg warmers will be just the thing to keep the cold at bay. Knit in an interesting rib pattern, you won't want to stop until both are ready to wear! Pair them with workout skirts and wear them to the gym until you get warmed up or pull them over skinny jeans, letting them slouch over Mary Janes or ballet flats for instant style.

FINISHED MEASUREMENTS

Circumference, unstretched and blocked:
   $10^1/_2$ in. (17 cm)
Length: 15 in. (38 cm)

YARN

Knit Picks Biggo; bulky weight #5 yarn; 50% superwash merino wool, 50% nylon; 110 yd. (100 m) and 3.5 oz. (100 g) per skein
   » 2 skeins Carnelian Heather

NEEDLES AND OTHER MATERIALS

   » U.S. 15 (10 mm) knitting needles
   » Tapestry needle

GAUGE

10 sts x 11 rows in pattern = 4 in. (10 cm)
Adjust needle size if necessary to obtain gauge.

Leg Warmer (Make 2)

CO 26 sts with cable CO or other stretchy CO.
Rows 1–8: K1, *k1 tbl, p1; rep from * to last st, k1.
Row 9: K1, *k2 tbl, p2; rep from * to last st, k1.
Repeat Row 9 for 9 in. (23 cm).
Repeat Rows 1–8 one time.
BO in pattern.

Finishing

Seam leg warmer with mattress stitch.
Weave in ends.

HEARTWARMING CUP SLEEVE

Design by Vikki Bird

he Heartwarming Cup Sleeve was designed for a friend who was having a wedding in the United Kingdom but lived in the United States and had requested only small gifts that she could easily take on the plane. Living in Florida, she and her husband have no need for my standard knitted gifts of hats and scarves and blankets, so I wondered what I could make instead. As my friend and I spent many of our formative years sitting chatting in coffee shops together, I decided on a matching pair of cup cozies.

FINISHED MEASUREMENTS

Top edge: 4³/₄ in. (12 cm)
Bottom edge: 4¹/₄ in. (10.5 cm)
Height: 2¹/₂ in. (6 cm)

YARN

Use a 100% wool yarn for its good insulating properties; the yarn should knit to standard Aran gauge (see Gauge) and should give good stitch definition.

- » 20 yd. (15 m) cream (MC)
- » 5 yd. (5 m) red (CC1)
- » 5 yd. (5 m) black (CC2)

NEEDLES AND OTHER MATERIALS

- » U.S. size 8 (5 mm) set of 4 or 5 double-pointed needles
- » Stitch marker
- » Tapestry needle

GAUGE

18 sts x 25 rows St st in the round = 4 in.
  (10 cm)
Adjust needle size if necessary to obtain gauge.

STITCH GUIDE

M1 (make 1): From the front, lift the loop between stitches with left needle, knit into back of loop.

NOTES

- » The cup sleeve is knitted in Aran weight yarn in the round, with the I♥U motif added at the end using Swiss darning. If you prefer, you could also work the chart in intarsia.
- » The pattern is written for double-pointed needles, but the magic loop technique using a single circular needle with a long cable may be used instead.

Pattern

Using MC, CO 38 sts. Join in the rnd, taking care not to twist the sts, and place a stitch marker at the start of the rnd.

Rnd 1: *K1, p1; rep from * to end of rnd. This row forms 1x1 rib.

Rep Rnd 1 two more times.

Next rnd: [M1, k19] twice—40 sts.

Work 3 rnds in St st (knit all sts).

Next rnd: [M1, k20] twice—42 sts.

Work 3 rnds in St st.

Next rnd: [M1, k21] twice—44 sts.

Work 3 rnds in 1x1 rib.

BO in pattern.

Heart Motif and Personalization

Flatten the cup cozy so that it lies with the increase sts running up either edge. Use duplicate stitch to apply the I♥U motif as indicated in the chart (the charted area corresponds to the area between the two ribbed sections).

To work duplicate stitch, bring the point of a needle threaded with yarn of the chosen color from back to front through the point of the V in the first stitch you want to duplicate. Pull the yarn through. Leave a few inches of yarn at the back of the work. To make the first "leg" of the V, put the needle in at the point at the right top of the V and out again at the top left of the V. Pull the yarn through. Then go back through the bottom point of the V where you started. This completes one duplicate stitch. Continue duplicating stitches until the pattern is complete.

Finishing

Weave in all ends and block as desired.

Heart Motif Chart

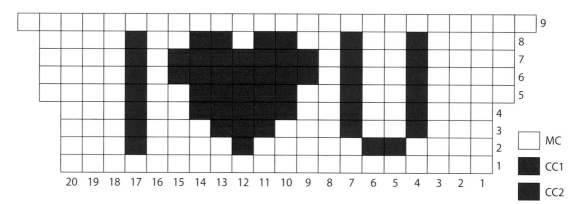

		MC
		CC1
		CC2

About Vikki Bird

Vikki Bird is a UK-based knitwear designer specializing in children's picture knits and slightly more conventional accessories for adults. Vikki is also an avid baker, seamstress, and bookworm.

PEACOCK TRAIL COWL

Design by Tessa Sweigert

*S*how off your style with this colorful cowl. I couldn't resist these beautiful jewel-tone yarns, reminiscent of a peacock. Have fun experimenting with color combinations for this quick knit. The bulky center of this cowl is sure to keep you warm, too!

FINISHED MEASUREMENTS

14.5 in. (37 cm) diameter x 7¹/₄ in. (18.5 cm) tall

YARN

Loops & Threads Cozy Wool; super bulky #6 yarn; 50% wool, 50% acrylic; 90 yd. (82 m) and 4.48 oz. (127 g) per skein
   » 1 skein #02237 Earth Tones (A)
Patons Cobbles; super bulky #6 yarn; 49% wool, 49% acrylic, 2% nylon; 41 yd. (37 m) and 3.5 oz. (100 g) per skein
   » 1 skein #85203 Tetra Teal (B)

NEEDLES AND OTHER MATERIALS

   » U.S. size 19 (15 mm) 16 in. (40 cm) circular needle
   » Tapestry needle

GAUGE

6 sts x 10 rows in St stitch, using B = 4 in. (10 cm)
Adjust needle size if necessary to obtain gauge.

NOTES

» In Rnds 5–13, all knit stitches are knit through the back loop.

» For a shorter, asymmetrical variation, start with Rnd 5 or bind off after Rnd 13.

Cowl

CO 48 sts with yarn A. Join to work in the round, being careful not to twist.

Rnd 1: *P1, k1; rep from * to end of rnd.

Rnd 2: *K1, sl 1 knitwise with yarn in back; rep from * to end of rnd.

Rnd 3: *K1, p1; rep from * to end of rnd.

Rnd 4: *Sl 1 knitwise with yarn in back, k1; rep from * to end of rnd.

Rnd 5: Pick up yarn B and knit all sts through the back loop.

Rnds 6–9: *P2, k4 tbl; rep from * to end of rnd.

Rnds 10–13: K2, *p2, k4 tbl; rep from * to last 4 sts, p2, k2 tbl.

Rnd 14: Pick up yarn A and knit all sts.

Rnd 15–18: Rep Rnds 1–4.

BO.

Finishing

Weave in ends and block.

About Tessa Sweigert

Tessa's inspiration and introduction to needlecrafts began at a young age, when her grandma taught her how to crochet. After several years experimenting in other artistic endeavors, she was inspired by a friend's projects to pull out her needles and hooks again. Her re-entry into the world of needle arts has led to an ever-growing stash of yarn and patterns. As her skills grew, friends challenged her to experiment with creating her own patterns and so began her new adventure as a knitwear designer.

When not knitting or working at her full-time job as a graphic designer, she feeds her creative curiosity with other crafts and hobbies such as photography, rug hooking, jewelry making, and drawing. She can often be found exploring art shows and antique stores. She also loves to spend time with family and friends, camping, hiking, or reading at her home in Mechanicsburg, Pennsylvania. She's rarely found without her other half, Mason, a dog who enjoys the outdoors and road trips as much as she does.

WINDING ROAD CONVERTIBLE COWL AND MITTS

Design by Carolyn Kern

The Winding Road Convertible Cowl and Mitts were inspired by the many chunky knit accessory pieces that have been gracing fashion runways in recent seasons. Yarn-over increases are used in the cowl version of the Winding Road stitch pattern to add interesting textural eyelet holes that have the added bonus of being quick and easy to execute. The yarn-over increases are replaced with make-1 increases in the mitts for a sleek and warm fit.

With the large scale of this piece, three additional yarn-over eyelet holes at the start of the final border become buttonholes for the three large buttons that are both decorative and functional. The convertible cowl can be buttoned in multiple ways for many great looks.

FINISHED MEASUREMENTS

8½ in. (21.6 cm) x 35 in. (89 cm)

YARN

» Bartlettyarns Fisherman 3-Ply Yarn; medium weight #4 yarn; 100% wool; 145 yd. (133 m) and 4 oz. (113 g) per skein
» 1 skein Spruce Heather

NEEDLES AND OTHER MATERIALS

» U.S. size 15 (10 mm) needles
» Three 1¾ in. (4.5 cm) diameter buttons
» Sewing needle and matching thread
» Tapestry needle
» Stitch markers

GAUGE

10½ sts in pattern stitch, after blocking = 4 in. (10 cm)

A gauge from 10–11 sts in 4 in. (10 cm) will result in the given finished measurements. Gauge is not critical for this project.

STITCH PATTERN

Winding Road Stitch Pattern—Cowl/ Eyelet Version (multiple of 9 sts)
Row 1 (RS): Yo, k2, ssk, k5.
Row 2 and all WS rows: Purl.
Row 3: K1, yo, k2, ssk, k4.
Row 5: K2, yo, k2, ssk, k3.
Row 7: K3, yo, k2, ssk, k2.
Row 9: K4, yo, k2, ssk, k1.
(continued on page 72)

WINDING ROAD CONVERTIBLE COWL

Row 11: K5, yo, k2, ssk.
Row 13: K5, k2tog, k2, yo.
Row 15: K4, k2tog, k2, yo, k1.
Row 17: K3, k2tog, k2, yo, k2.
Row 19: K2, k2tog, k2, yo, k3.
Row 21: K1, k2tog, k2, yo, k4.
Row 23: K2tog, k2, yo, k5.
Row 24: Purl.
Repeat Rows 1–24 for pattern.

Cowl

CO 22 sts.
Knit 3 rows.
Set-up row: K2, pm, k18, pm, k2.
Next row (RS): K2, sm, work two 9-st repeats of Winding Road Stitch Pattern Row 1, sm, k2.
Next row: K2, sm, work two 9-st repeats of Winding Road Stitch Pattern Row 2, sm, k2.
Continue as established, knitting 2 sts at the beginning and end of each row, and following Winding Road Stitch Pattern between markers through Row 24.
Repeat Rows 1–24 of stitch pattern 3 more times, removing markers on the last row. The piece should measure approximately 33 in. (84 cm), unblocked.
Buttonhole row: K2, k2tog, yo, k5, k2tog, yo, k6, k2tog, yo, k3.
Knit 3 rows.
BO in purl on RS.

Finishing

Weave in yarn ends. Sew buttons to end opposite buttonholes. Use buttonholes as a guide for button locations.

As with most knitting, hand washing is the best way to block the Winding Road Convertible Cowl. Lay the piece flat to air dry, smoothing it into a rectangular shape. If you are in a hurry to wear it (and you have used the Bartlettyarns Fisherman 3-Ply or another wool yarn), a light pressing with a steam iron will also work well. (Please remember never to use a steam iron on synthetic fibers.)

Button the cowl in any way you dream up and then rotate it about your neck until it just feels right.

Winding Road Stitch Pattern—Cowl/Eyelet Version

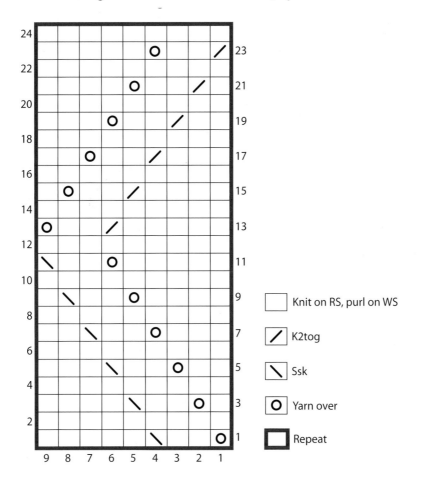

Knit on RS, purl on WS

/ K2tog

\ Ssk

O Yarn over

Repeat

About Carolyn Kern

Carolyn Kern is a knitwear designer and Craft Yarn Council of America certified knitting instructor who manages to also find time to pursue a career in engineering. Her designs have been published by *Interweave Knits*, *Knitscene*, *Mollie Makes*, Quince & Co, Blue Moon Fiber Arts, and Manos del Uruguay.

WINDING ROAD MITTS

FINISHED MEASUREMENTS

Hand circumference: 7 in. (17.8 cm)
Height: 7¹/₂ in. (19 cm)

YARN

Bartlettyarns Fisherman 3-Ply Yarn; medium
weight #4 yarn; 100% wool; 145 yd. (133 m)
and 4 oz. (113 g) per skein
  » 1 skein Spruce Heather *Project usage:
    approximately 73 yd. (67 m)*

NEEDLES AND OTHER MATERIALS

  » U.S. size 11 (8 mm) set of double-
    pointed needles
  » Waste yarn
  » Tapestry needle

GAUGE

12 sts in pattern stitch, blocked = 4 in.
  (10 cm)
Adjust needle size if necessary to obtain gauge.

NOTES

» The right and left mitt are identical.
» The entire chart is worked one time for each mitt.
» The mitts are knit in the round on double-pointed needles or, if you prefer, two circular needles or a long circular magic loop needle.

STITCH GUIDE

M1L (make-1 left slant): Using right needle, lift the yarn between stitches in last row, entering from the back. Pass it to left needle and knit it through the back.

M1R (make-1 right slant): Using right needle, lift the yarn between stitches in last row, entering from the front. Pass it to left needle and knit it through the front.

Mitt (Make 2)

CO 19. Join to work in the rnd.

Knit 1 rnd.

Work Rnds 1–32 of Winding Road Stitch Pattern Chart, slipping thumb sts to waste yarn in Row 20, or follow written instructions, as follows:

Rnd 1: K1, M1R, k2, ssk, k9, k2tog, k2, M1L, k1.

Rnds 2, 4, 6, 8, and 10: Knit.

Rnd 3: K2, M1R, k2, ssk, k7, k2tog, k2, M1L, k2.

Rnd 5: K3, M1R, k2, ssk, k5, k2tog, k2, M1L, k3.

Rnd 7: K4, M1R, k2, ssk, k3, k2tog, k2, M1L, k4.

Rnd 9: K4, k2tog, k2, M1L, k1, M1L, k1, M1R, k1, M1R, k2, ssk, k4.

Rnd 11: K3, k2tog, k2, M1L, k7, M1R, k2, ssk, k3.

Rnd 12: K9, M1L, k3, M1R, k9.

Rnd 13: K2, k2tog, k2, M1L, k11, M1R, k2, ssk, k2.

Rnds 14 and 16: Knit.

Rnd 15: K1, k2tog, k2, M1L, k4, M1L, k5, M1R, k4, M1R, k2, ssk, k1.

Rnd 17: K1, M1R, k2, ssk, k15, k2tog, k2, M1L, k1.

Rnd 18: K9, M1L, k7, M1R, k9.

Rnd 19: K2, M1R, k2, ssk, k15, k2tog, k2, M1L, k2.

Rnd 20: K11, slip next 7 sts to waste yarn for thumb, k11—22 sts.

Rnd 21: K3, M1R, k2, ssk, k6, k2tog, k2, M1L, k3.

Rnds 22, 24, 26, 28, and 30: Knit.

Rnd 23: K4, M1R, k2, ssk, k4, k2tog, k2, M1L, k4.

Rnd 25: K4, k2tog, k2, M1L, K4, M1R, k2, ssk, k4.

Rnd 27: K3, k2tog, k2, M1L, k6, M1R, k2, ssk, k3.

Rnd 29: K2, k2tog, k2, M1L, K8, M1R, k2, ssk, k2.

Rnd 31: K1, k2tog, k2, M1L, k10, M1R, k2, ssk, k1.

Rnd 32: Knit.

Loosely BO all sts.

Thumb

Place thumb sts on dpns. Joining yarn, pick up 2 sts at intersection of mitt and top of thumb—9 sts.

Knit 4 rnds.

Loosely BO all sts.

Finishing

Weave in yarn ends.

As with most knitting, hand washing is the best way to block the Winding Road Mitts. Lay them flat to air dry. Of course, mitts may be worn without blocking.

Winding Road Stitch Pattern—Mitt Version

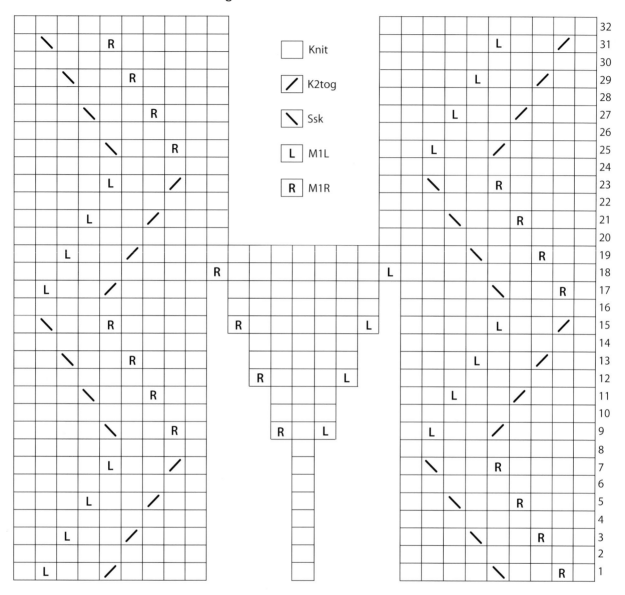

Work from the bottom up, all rounds from right to left.

SWIRL SET NECKLACE AND BRACELET

Design by Helena Callum

This necklace and bracelet are formed using a simple braid of three I-cords and a pretty swirly clasp to finish each piece. The end caps of the clasps used here have an internal diameter of about 1/4 in. (6 mm), and although they are designed for use in kumihimo jewelry making, this size makes them perfect for knitted I-cord too. Make the most of the clasp by wearing the necklace with the clasp towards the front!

FINISHED MEASUREMENTS

For Bracelet (Necklace)
Overall length including clasp: 8 (21) in./21 (54) cm
Length of braided section: 6 (19) in./16 (49) cm
Width: 3/4 (3/4) in./2 (2) cm

YARN

Libby Summers Chunky Yarn; bulky weight #5 yarn; 100% Peruvian Highland wool; 54.5 yd. (50 m) and 1.7 oz. (50 g) per skein
» 1 ball #434 Qulqi (light gray marl; MC)
» 1 ball #860 Anqas (blue; CC)

NEEDLES AND OTHER MATERIALS

» U.S. size 6 (4 mm) double-pointed needles
» 2 swirl clasps, 3/4 in. (18 mm) diameter
» PVA (white) glue
» Cyanoacrylate glue (super glue)
» 3 safety pins or small stitch holders

GAUGE

18 rows measured over 2-st I-cord = 4 in. (10 cm)
I-cord diameter = 1/4 in. (6 mm)
Adjust needle size if necessary to obtain gauge.

NOTES

» The bracelet and necklace are worked in the same way; the only difference between them is the length.
» The swirl clasps are widely available online: search for "kumihimo swirl clasp." Clasp vendors will also stock cyanoacrylate glue.
» Untangle the working ends of the yarn as you braid the I-cords. They do get tangled, but it is worth keeping the yarn connected as you may need to increase the length of the I-cords.

STITCH GUIDE

I-cord: Use two dpns. CO the specified number of sts. *Knit the sts, but do not turn your work at the end of the row. Slide the sts to the other end of the same needle, pull the working yarn behind the sts in preparation to knit the first st again. Rep from * until the I-cord is the required length.

Knitted cast-on: Insert tip of RH needle into st as if to knit, wrap yarn and pull through a new st. Place new st on the LH needle.

Purled cast-on: Insert tip of RH needle into st as if to purl, wrap yarn and pull through a new st. Place new st on the LH needle.

Pattern—Bracelet (Necklace)

Note: When only one number is given, it is the same for both bracelet and necklace.

With CC, CO 2 sts.

Work I-cord for 5 rows.

Slide the sts to the working end of the needle as if to continue the I-cord.

Inc row 1 (RS): CO 2 sts using the knitted cast-on method, k4—4 sts.

Inc row 2: CO 2 sts using the purled cast-on method, p2, slip the 2 sts just worked back to the LH needle—6 sts.

Turn the work so that the RS is facing you. Place 2 sts at the LH end onto a safety pin or stitch holder, place 2 sts at the RH end onto a safety pin or stitch holder—2 sts.

With CC, continue to work in I-cord until the I-cord measures 8 (22½) in./20 (57) cm from the level of the additional cast-on sts. Place the 2 sts onto a safety pin or stitch holder. Do not break the yarn.

With RS facing, transfer the 2 sts from the safety pin or stitch holder at RH end to a dpn—2 sts.

Join MC and work in I-cord until the I-cord measures 8 (22$\frac{1}{2}$) in./20 (57) cm. Place the 2 sts onto a safety pin or stitch holder. Do not break yarn.

With RS facing, transfer the 2 sts from the safety pin or stitch holder at LH end to a dpn—2 sts.

Using the other end of the ball, join MC and work in I-cord until the I-cord measures 8 (22$\frac{1}{2}$) in./20 (57) cm. Place the 2 sts onto a safety pin or stitch holder. Do not break yarn.

Weave in the MC ends at the start of the MC I-cords, ensuring that each join is neat. With RS facing and the 3 I-cords hanging toward you, pin the start of the work to a surface such as a cork board or carpet. Braid the 3 I-cords together firmly and evenly.

Measure braided section: It should be approximately 6$\frac{1}{4}$ (19$\frac{1}{4}$) in./16 (49) cm long and end with the CC I-cord in the middle. If necessary, work more rows of I-cord.

With RS facing, place the 6 sts on a dpn with the CC sts in the middle. For each pair of sts the working yarn will be at the LH st.

Turn the work so that the WS is facing, continue with CC.

Set-up row (WS): Sl 4 purlwise, p2.

Dec row 1: BO 2 sts, knit to end—4 sts.

Dec row 2: BO 2 sts purlwise, sl st on RH needle to LH needle—2 sts.

With RS facing, continue I-cord for 5 rows.

BO. Break the rem ends of yarn.

Finishing

Arrange the braiding so that it is even, then weave in the ends.

Stiffen the unbraided I-cord ends by saturating them with PVA glue. Work PVA glue in with your fingers and leave to dry overnight.

Trim the stiffened ends to fit into the end caps, noting that the two end caps are different lengths.

Following the directions on the cyanoacrylate glue pack, carefully glue the I-cord into the end caps of the clasp, ensuring that the two parts of the clasp are properly aligned. Allow to dry before wearing.

About Helena Callum

Helena Callum lives in southern Scotland, UK. She enjoys knitting and designing accessories such as socks, gloves, bags and jewelry.

REALEZA COWL

Design by Sarah Sundermeyer

*T*he color and velvety texture of this cowl remind me of the rich cloth that often adorns kings and queens, and so the cowl is named after the Spanish word for royalty. Knit in scrumptious Malabrigo Rasta, it sits close to your neck for extra coziness in the winter. Simple braided cables are spaced evenly around the cowl, and they alternate going up and down to add interest as you are knitting. The luxuriousness of the cowl will make you feel like royalty whenever you wear it.

FINISHED MEASUREMENTS

Circumference: 22 in. (56 cm), blocked
Height: 8 in. (20 cm), blocked

YARN

Malabrigo Rasta; super bulky weight #6 yarn; 100% merino wool; 90 yd. (82 m) and 5.3 oz. (150 g) per skein
» 1 skein Baya Electrica

NEEDLES AND OTHER MATERIALS

» U.S. size 15 (10 mm) 16 in. (40 cm) circular needle
» Stitch marker
» Cable needle

GAUGE

9 sts x 15 rows in St st = 4 in. (10 cm)
Adjust needle size if necessary to obtain gauge.

STITCH GUIDE

C4B (cable 4 back): Slip 2 sts onto cable needle and hold to back, k2 from left-hand needle, k2 from cable needle.

C4F (cable 4 front): Slip 2 sts onto cable needle and hold to front, k2 from left-hand needle, k2 from cable needle.

Cowl

CO 54 sts. Join in the round and place marker, being careful not to twist your sts.

Border
Rnd 1: Purl.
Rnd 2: Knit.
Rnd 3: Purl.

Cables
Set-up rnd: *K6, p3; rep from * to end of round.
Rep set-up rnd once more, then move on to the cable pattern.
Rnd 1: *C4B, k2, p3, C4F, k2, p3; rep from * to end of rnd.
Rnd 2: *K6, p3; rep from * to end of rnd.
Rnd 3: *K2, C4F, p3, k2, C4B, p3; rep from * to end of rnd.
Rnd 4: *K6, p3; rep from * to end of rnd.
Rep Rnds 1–4 five times total.
Next rnd: *K6, p3; rep from * to end of rnd.

Border
Rnd 1: Purl.
Rnd 2: Knit.
Rnd 3: Purl.
BO all sts knitwise.

Finishing
Weave in ends and block.

CAVENDISH CUFF

Design by Brenda Castiel

*W*hat does your outfit need to make it special? A casual fiber or fabric accessory like a knitted cuff! Cavendish is the perfect lacy accent for a pretty wrist or ankle. Wear it to a summer party, a barbeque, or a wedding.

FINISHED MEASUREMENTS

Approximately 4$^{1}/_{2}$ x 8$^{1}/_{2}$ in. (11.5 x 21.5 cm)

YARN

Handmaiden Fine Yarn Mini Maiden; super fine weight #1 yarn; 50% wool, 50% silk; 546 yd. (499 m) and 3.5 oz. (100 g) per skein

» 1 skein Ivory *Project usage: approximately 137 yd. (125 m)*

NEEDLES AND OTHER MATERIALS

» U.S. size 5 (3.75 mm) knitting needles
» U.S. F (3.75 mm) crochet hook
» 2 buttons
» Yarn needle

GAUGE

24 sts x 32 rows in St st = 4 in. (10 cm)
Adjust needle size if necessary to obtain gauge.

NOTES

» Chart shows RS rows only.

Cuff

CO 49 sts.

Set-up row 1: Sl 1 knitwise, p1, k1, p1, k41, [p1, k1] twice.

Set-up row 2: Sl 1 purlwise, k1, p1, k1, k41, [k1, p1] twice.

Row 1 (RS): Sl 1 knitwise, p1, k1, p1, p41 sts, [p1, k1] twice.

Row 2: Sl 1 purlwise, k1, p1, k1, p41 sts, [k1, p1] twice.

Continue in pattern until Row 29 of Cavendish Lace Chart is complete.

Row 30 (WS): Sl 1 purlwise, k1, p1, k1, k41, [k1, p1] twice.

Row 31: Sl 1 knitwise, p1, k1, p1, k41, [p1, k1] twice.

BO all sts, but do not cut yarn. Slip remaining st to crochet hook. Work single crochet along short edge of work (working approximately 1 single crochet in every row) as follows: Single crochet evenly across first $^3/_4$ in (2 cm), chain 8 for button loop, single crochet along edge to $^3/_4$ in. (2 cm) before end of piece, chain 8 for button loop, single crochet along edge to end. Break yarn and draw through last st, pull tight.

Finishing

Weave in all loose ends and block. Sew on buttons opposite of button loops.

Cavendish Lace Chart

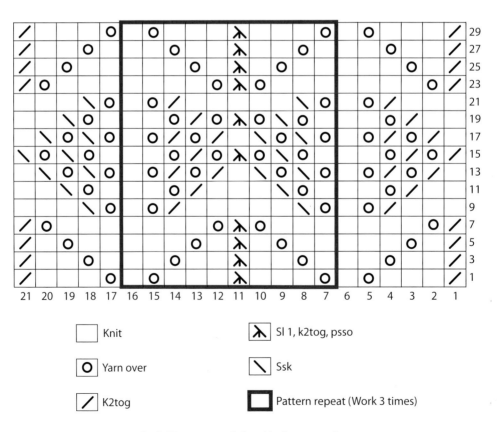

On WS rows, purl the 41 chart stitches.

STRANDED STRIPED MITTS

Design by Erica Mount

__T__hese mitts wrap your hands in striking stripes and keep them toasty while leaving your fingers free for typing, texting, or knitting. Use high-contrast colors for bold stripes or a lighter and darker shade of the same color for a softer look.

FINISHED MEASUREMENTS

Length: 7 in. (17.5 cm)
Width: 4 in. (10 cm)

YARN

Cascade Yarns Cascade 220; medium weight #4 yarn; 100% wool; 220 yd. (201 m) and 3.5 oz. (100 g) per skein
   » 1 skein Mallard (MC)
   » 1 skein Silver Grey (CC)

NEEDLES AND OTHER MATERIALS

   » U.S. size 8 (5 mm) dpns or circular needle
   » Tapestry needle
   » Stitch markers (optional)
   » Scrap yarn or stitch holder

GAUGE

16 sts x 20 rows = 4 in. (10 cm)
Adjust needle size if necessary to obtain gauge.

NOTES

» The mitts are reversible, so just make two exactly the same.

» When working stranded colorwork, knit each stitch in the color indicated by the chart. When not using a color, carry it along the back of the work. Pick it up again when you need to use it. This will form strands of yarn (floats) on the back of the work. Catch floats by wrapping the yarns around each other when there are more than 3 stitches in a row of a single color. This will prevent long floats on the back of the work.

» All increases in this pattern are backwards loop increases so that the surrounding sts are not distorted.

STITCH GUIDE

Backwards loop increase: Twist the working yarn into a loop (twist clockwise for left-leaning increase and counterclockwise for right-leaning increase), slip the loop onto the right hand needle, and pull tight.

Mitt (Make 2)

With MC, CO 32 sts. Join in the round, being careful not to twist.

Rnds 1–2: *K2, p2; rep from * to end of rnd.

Rnd 3: Knit.

Rnd 4: With CC, knit all sts.

Rnds 5–6: With MC, knit all sts.

Rnds 7–29: Knit the Stranded Colorwork Chart, working from right to left and bottom to top. Please note the following specific instructions for Rnds 12 and 22:

On **Rnd 12,** st 16 becomes the center of the thumb gusset. Increases are done on each side of this st.

On **Rnd 22,** increase by 1 st after st 15, then slip the following 11 thumb gusset sts onto scrap yarn or a stitch holder and continue knitting to the end of the chart.

Rnds 30–31: With MC, knit all sts.

Rnd 32: With CC, knit all sts.

Rnd 33: With MC, knit all sts.

Rnds 34–35: *K2, p2; rep from * to end of rnd.

BO in k2, p2 pattern.

Thumb

Pick up 11 sts from scrap yarn. Pick up 3 more sts in the gap where the thumb meets the hand—14 sts.

Rnd 1: K2tog, knit until 2 sts rem, k2tog—12 sts.

Rnd 2: *K2, p2; rep from * to end of rnd.

BO in k2, p2 pattern.

About Erica Mount

Erica Mount enjoys objects that are both beautiful and useful, which is why she focuses her gorgeous colorwork designs on mittens. Just about everyone can use a pair of mittens, and they are also very visible, so intricate work doesn't end up hidden under a coat or shoe.

Stranded Colorwork Chart

Legend:
- Mallard
- Silver Grey
- **M1L** Make 1 left
- **M1R** Make 1 right

INSTANT GRATIFICATION COWL

Design by Dana Gervais

This cowl is a quick, gratifying knit that makes a great last-minute gift or a luxurious indulgence for yourself. It uses one skein of bulky weight yarn and feels soft and warm against the skin. A simple two-row pattern repeat makes this a great beginner project or a quick stash buster for more experienced knitters.

FINISHED MEASUREMENTS

49 x 14 in. (124.5 x 35 cm), measured after
  blocking, flat, before seaming

YARN

Cascade Elite Yarns Wynter; bulky weight
#5 yarn; 50% superfine alpaca, 50% wool;
120 yd. (110 m) and 3.5 oz. (100 g) per skein
  » 1 skein #7631 Jacaranda

NEEDLES AND OTHER MATERIALS

  » U.S. size 15 (10 mm) knitting needles
  » Tapestry needle

GAUGE

2 sts x 4 rows in pattern stitch, blocked =
  4 in. (10 cm)

*The nature of this stitch pattern and the nature
of the alpaca content of the yarn result in a very
stretchy finished project. The cowl will stretch
significantly lengthwise when blocked and will
result in a cowl that is longer and narrower than
when bound off. Obtaining the given gauge is not
crucial for a successful project but will affect the
finished measurements and the amount of yarn
needed. Adjust needle size if necessary to obtain
gauge.*

Cowl

CO 25 sts.

Row 1: Knit all sts, wrapping the yarn twice
  around the needle.

Row 2: Knit all sts, dropping the extra wrap on
  each stitch.

Rep Rows 1–2 until you have 2 yd. (2 m) of yarn
  left or scarf is as long as you would like.

Bind off all sts loosely, leaving a long tail approximately 18 in. (45 cm).

Finishing

Using a tapestry needle and yarn tail from bind-off
  edge, seam the bind-off edge and the cast-on
  edge together. Alternatively, for a Mobius-style
  cowl twist the scarf once before seaming the
  edges together.

Weave in all ends. Block.

FAST FINGERLESS MITTS

Design by Ellen Harvey

__T__he color-changing yarn does the work to make this simple pair of mitts special.

FINISHED MEASUREMENTS

8 in. (20.25 cm) wide x 6$\frac{1}{2}$ in. (16.5 cm) long, measured flat before seaming

YARN

Berroco Lodge; bulky weight #5 yarn; 47% wool, 47% acrylic, 6% rayon; 98 yd. (90 m) and 1.7 oz. (50 g) per skein
  » 1 skein #7452 Jackson Lake

NEEDLES AND OTHER MATERIALS

  » U.S. size 9 (5.5 mm) knitting needles
  » U.S. size 10 (6 mm) knitting needles
  » Tapestry needle

GAUGE

4 sts in St st with size 10 (6 mm) needles = 1 in. (2.5 cm)
Adjust needle size if necessary to obtain gauge.

NOTES

  » Mitts are knitted flat and then seamed, leaving an opening for the thumb.

Mitt (Make 2)

With smaller needles, CO 32 sts.

Work in k2, p2 rib for 1¼ in. (3 cm).

Change to larger needles and work in St st for 4 in. (10 cm).

Work in k2, p2 rib for 1¼ in. (3 cm) for top of mitt.

BO all sts in pattern.

Finishing

Seam 4 in. (10 cm) from cuff to thumb opening. Seam top 1 in. (2.5 cm) of ribbing.

Block if desired. Weave in all ends.

COLORBLOCK WALLET

Design by Faye Kennington

A zippered pouch always comes in handy. This retro-inspired colorblock wallet is the perfect size pencil case, make-up bag, or notions organizer. It knits up quickly and gives you a chance to try stranded knitting, felting, and sewing in a zipper without making a big investment.

FINISHED MEASUREMENTS

Approximately 8½ in. (21 cm) long x 4 in. (10 cm) high

YARN

Knit Picks Wool of the Andes; medium weight #4 yarn; 100% wool; 110 yd. (100 m) and 1.7 oz. (50 g) per skein
  » Amethyst Heather (MC)
  » Cloud (CCA)
  » Conch (CCB)
or
  » Mink Heather (MC)
  » Marina (CCA)
  » Cloud (CCB)
Note: You will need 37 yd. (34 m) each of three different colors of 100% wool (not superwash) worsted weight yarn.

NEEDLES AND OTHER MATERIALS

  » U.S. 10½ (6.5 mm) knitting needles
  » Tapestry needle
  » Iron
  » Sewing needle and thread
  » Sharp-tipped scissors
  » Straight pins (optional)
  » 9 in. (23 cm) zipper
  » 1 in. (2.5 cm) button

GAUGE

14 sts x 18 rows in St st, after felting = 4 in. (10 cm)
Adjust needle size if necessary to obtain gauge.

NOTES

  » You may want to try felting test swatches of your yarn selections to ensure they felt consistently in size. Different brands and different dyes can impact the felting process.

COLORWORK KNITTING TIPS

Adjust the tension of the carried yarn at the end of each row, if necessary. The carries should lie flat without being taut when the stitches are well stretched out across the needle.

Twist the yarns the st before a color change. To twist the yarn, you need only lift the alternate color yarn over the one being worked to form a link.

If a twist shows on the right side of the knitting, it can usually be pulled to the back of the work by tugging gently on both sides of the carry on the wrong side.

At the end of every row, untwist the working yarn.

Pattern

CO 30 sts with CCA.
Work instructions below or from chart.
Work 4 rows 1x1 ribbing (k1, p1).
Work 6 rows St st (knit 1 row, purl 1 row) starting with RS row.

Color Block 1

Row 11 (RS): K28 with CCA, with CCB k2.
Row 12 (WS): P4 with CCB, with CCA p26.
Next row (RS): Knit to 2 sts before color change in previous row with CCA, with CCB knit to end.
Next row (WS): Purl to 2 sts after color change in previous row with CCB, with CCA purl to end.
Work previous 2 rows 5 more times.
With CCB, work 10 rows St st, starting with RS row.

Color Block 2

Row 35 (RS): With MC k2, with CCB k28.
Row 36 (WS): P26 with CCB, with MC p4.
Next row (RS): Knit to 2 sts after color change in previous row with MC, with CCB knit to end.

Next row (WS): Purl to 2 sts before color change in previous row with CCB, with MC purl to end.
Work previous 2 rows 5 more times.
With MC, work 5 rows St st, starting and ending with RS row.

Flap Closure

Row 54 (WS): K3, purl to last 3 sts, k3.
Row 55 (RS): Knit.
Work previous 2 rows once more.
Row 58 (WS): K3, purl to last 6 sts, k3, w&t.
Row 59 (RS): Knit.
Next row (WS): K3, purl to last 6 sts before w&t of previous row, k3, w&t.
Next row (RS): Knit.
Work previous 2 rows 5 more times.
Next row (WS): K6, w&t.
Next row (RS): Knit.
Next row: K3, w&t.
Next row: Knit.
Next 2 rows: Knit all 30 sts.
BO all sts and cut yarn.

Finishing

Seaming

With RS facing, fold CO edge up to meet first row of the Flap Closure, marked with the first set of purl bumps on edges. Whipstitch sides of wallet closed on WS. Weave in loose ends. Turn wallet RS out.

Felting

Felt wallet until it measures approximately $8\frac{1}{2}$ in. (21 cm) long by 4 in. (10 cm) high with flap folded over. Several ways to do this can be found on the Internet. My favorite way is to put the wallet into a top-loading washing machine and run a small hot water load with a bit of laundry soap. The washing machine and hot water will do all the agitating necessary to felt the wallet and you can remove the wallet periodically to check to make sure it is felted to the correct size.

The wallet length must be 9 in. (23 cm) or less. Block the wallet to have nice square corners and sharp angles using an iron on steam setting.

Adding the Zipper

Using thread and sewing needle, whipstitch the zipper into the wallet with closed end under wider end of flap and zipper head end on narrow end of flap. Using straight pins to pin the zipper evenly to the wallet prior to sewing may help prevent the knitting from stretching as you sew (which distorts the finished object). *Note:* The zipper is slightly longer than the finished wallet. The excess zipper on the closed end can be tucked into the wallet. The zipper need only be sewn on the long edges to the sides of the wallet.

Adding the Button

Sew the button to the front side of the wallet under the wide section of the flap. It should be centered about $1\frac{1}{2}$ in. (4 cm) from the bottom fold and 1 in. (2.5 cm) from the right side. Fold the flap over the button to find the correct spot for the buttonhole. Use the sharp point of the scissors to make a small snip to start the buttonhole. Carefully snip the buttonhole edge slightly larger until it can be worked over the button. Felted knitting won't unravel!

Colorblock Wallet

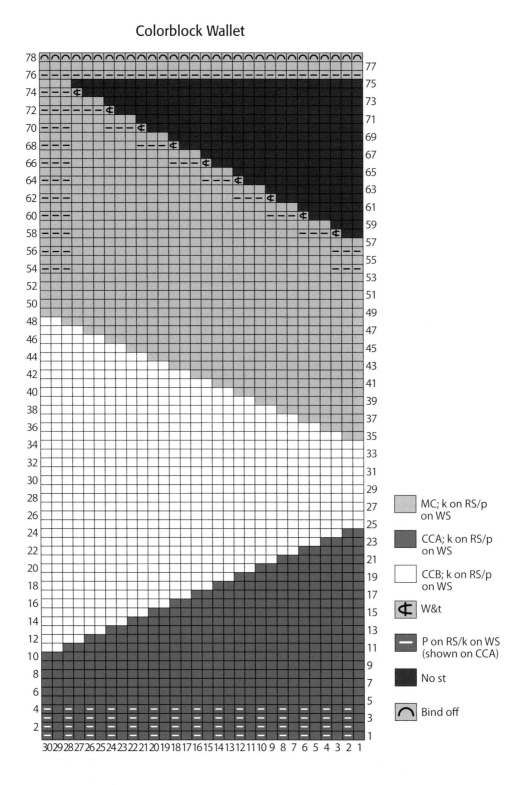

MC; k on RS/p on WS

CCA; k on RS/p on WS

CCB; k on RS/p on WS

⊄ W&t

— P on RS/k on WS (shown on CCA)

No st

⌒ Bind off

COLOR ME ADVENTUROUS
SHAWLETTE

Design by Sandra Ronca

This stylish piece can be worn with the buttons front or back—it is an eye-catcher either way, and it will keep the shoulders warm on all kinds of adventures. You can wear it with a blouse, T-shirt, tank top, or camisole, and it will fit under a jacket easily.

Geometrically speaking, this shawlette is an upside-down isosceles triangle with a piece missing in the middle of the top part, like a letter V. You will start knitting at the bottom point of the triangle. The buttons (two or four) will be lined up along the right side of the top edge; the buttonholes will be on the left side.

FINISHED MEASUREMENTS

Folded over, it will be approximately 18 in. (45 cm) wide in the shoulders with up to 4 in. (10 cm) of ease and 10 in. (25 cm) high from points to neckline.

YARN

Malabrigo Rastita; light weight #3 yarn; 100% merino wool; 310 yd. (283 m) and 3.5 oz. (100 g) per skein
  » 1 skein #132 No Me Olvides

NEEDLES AND OTHER MATERIALS

  » U.S. size 13 (9 mm) knitting needles
  » ³/₄ to 1 in. (2 to 2.5 cm) lightweight buttons

GAUGE

9 sts x 23 rows in garter st = 4 in. (10 cm)
Adjust needle size if necessary to obtain gauge.

NOTES

  » You'll be using a rather large needle with a relatively small yarn. The fabric is supposed to be very loose, so don't be alarmed.
  » It is highly recommended to choose lightweight buttons.
  » This shawlette is worked in garter stitch with a chain edge. The increase is created by yarn overs. The neckline is created by partial bind-offs from the inside out.
  » The pattern is suitable for adventurous beginners because of the stitch repetitions, but there's some shaping involved.

Shawlette

You will now be knitting the basic triangle.

CO 3 sts.

Row 1: K1, yo, knit to end.

Row 2: Sl 1 purlwise, yo, knit to end.

Rep Row 2 until there are 80 sts on the needle.

Next row: S1 1 purlwise, yo, k34, BO 10, knit to end.

You will now continue knitting the left side of the collar, leaving all stitches on the other side of the partial BO to rest on your needle.

Left Side

Row 1: Sl 1 purlwise, yo, knit to end.

Row 2: Sl 1 knitwise, BO 1 (including slipped st), knit to end.

Rep Rows 1–2 eight more times.

Row 19 (for 2 buttonholes): Sl 1 purlwise, k12, [yo, k2tog, k9] twice.

or

Row 19 (for 4 buttonholes): Sl 1 purlwise, k4, [yo, k2tog, k6] 3 times, yo, k2tog, k4.

Row 20: Sl 1 purlwise, knit to end.

Row 21: Sl 1 knitwise, BO (including slipped st), cut yarn, weave in ends.

You will now reattach the yarn on the inside of the right side of the collar, where the partial BO started.

Right Side

Row 1: Sl 1 knitwise, BO 1 (including slipped st), knit to end.

Row 2: Sl 1 purlwise, yo, knit to end.

Rep Rows 1–2 nine more times.

Row 21: Sl 1 knitwise, BO (including slipped st), cut yarn, weave in all ends.

Finishing

Sew on buttons as shown on page 105. Reinforce buttonholes with whipstitches, if necessary. Wash and block carefully to achieve desired measurements. It is recommended to stretch the fabric more horizontally than vertically to make it hug the shoulders.

About Sandra Ronca

Sandra Ronca learned to knit and crochet from both of her grandmothers when she was just a little kid. They kindled her interest with new patterns and challenging projects until she was thoroughly hooked. When she moved to the United States from Germany in 2012, she found herself in the lucky position to have the head space and time to pursue her hobbies and indulge her passions, like knitting.

In 2015, Sandra founded a giving circle of knitters called Craft Around Corners. The group knits and donates mainly hot-and-cold packs designed by her. The group's name plays off the idiom "think around corners," because crafty people are clever!

SEWING BUTTONS ONTO LOOSELY KNIT FABRIC

1. Hone in on a stitch you want to sew the button to. Imagine the stitch being a square with the purl nub as the top, the two sides of the loop as the sides, and the upper part of the stitch below as the bottom of the square. Bring the thread through the stitch from the wrong side.

2. Weave thread around the top of the stitch.

3. Weave the thread around the right side of the stitch.

4. Weave the thread through the button.

5. Weave the thread around the bottom of the stitch. Pull the button close to the fabric (not shown in photo for demonstration purposes).

6. Weave the thread around the right side of the stitch and bring the thread back to the wrong side of the fabric. Weave in ends.

OCEAN CITY BOOT CUFFS

Design by Christen Comer

hese boot cuffs are knit up quickly with a bulky yarn (or worsted weight with two strands held together) and big needles; once you cast on, the knitting will coast along. With such a quick project, take the time to add special details or try a new technique: Instead of seaming, add toggles to connect the cuffs. Or try a provisional cast-on and graft the cuff closed with Kitchener stitch. If you want to add buttons, they could be purely decorative or you could add small crocheted loops after binding off and make them functional. The world is your oyster!

FINISHED MEASUREMENTS

5 in. (13 cm) high; circumference will be determined by the number of rows knitted (sample is 7 in. [18 cm] circumference)

YARN

Red Heart Unforgettable; medium weight #4 yarn; 100% acrylic; 270 yd. (247 m) and 3.5 oz. (100 g) per skein
   » 1 skein Tidal

NEEDLES AND OTHER MATERIALS

   » U.S. size 10½ (6.5 mm) knitting needles

GAUGE

19 sts x 24 rows = 4 in. (10 cm)
Adjust needle size if necessary to obtain gauge.

STITCH GUIDE

C4B (cable 4 back): Slip 2 sts onto cable needle and hold to back, k2 from left-hand needle, k2 from cable needle.
C4F (cable 4 front): Slip 2 sts onto cable needle and hold to front, k2 from left-hand needle, k2 from cable needle.

Cuff (Make 2)

Follow chart or written directions, as follows.
With preferred method, CO 26 sts.

Row 1 (RS): P6, k14, p6.

Row 2: Purl.

Row 3: Knit.

Row 4: K6, p14, k6.

Row 5: P6, k2, [C4B] 3 times, p6.

Row 6: Purl.

Row 7: K6, [C4B] 3 times, k8.

Row 8: K6, p14, k6.

Row 9: P6, k2, [C4B] 3 times, p6.

Row 10: Purl.

Row 11: K10, [C4B] twice, k8.

Row 12: K6, p14, k6.

Row 13: P6, [C4F] twice, k6, p6.

Row 14: Purl.

Row 15: K8, [C4F] twice, k10.

Row 16: K6, p14, k6.

Rep Rows 5–16 until desired width.

Finishing

If you plan to seam ends normally or use toggles, bind off knitwise. If using a provisional cast-on and invisible seam, pick up cast-on stitches and bind off using Kitchener stitch. Block lightly.

Attach buttons or toggles and/or add crochet chain button loops, if desired.

Ocean City Chart

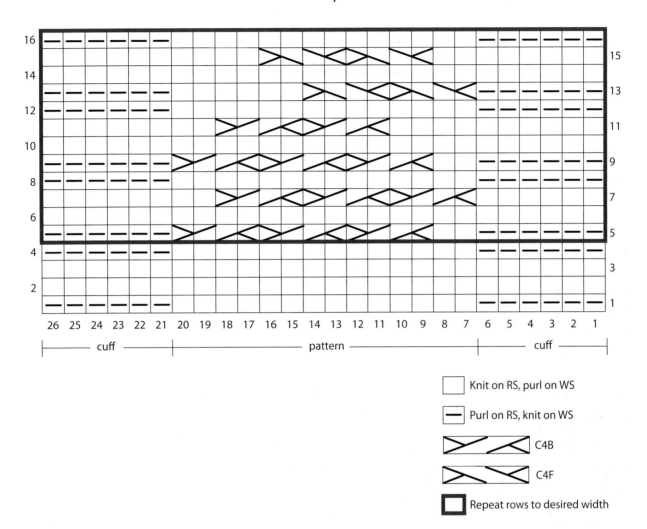

Knit on RS, purl on WS

— Purl on RS, knit on WS

C4B

C4F

Repeat rows to desired width

MARY JETTS

Design by Christen Comer

These quick-knit slippers will serve you well in cold winter months! A cuff around the ankle ensures they can't slip off, and a reverse stockinette sole means comfort on the inside. Make several pairs to keep, or give them away as easy, warm, and fun gifts!

SIZES

Women's Small (Large), based on ankle and foot circumference; the length can be adjusted to desired foot length as you work.

YARN

Loops & Threads Cozy Wool; super bulky #6 yarn; 50% wool, 50% acrylic; 90 yd. (82 m) and 4.48 oz. (127 g) per skein
» 1 skein Clematis

NEEDLES AND OTHER MATERIALS

» U.S. size 13 (9 mm) needles

GAUGE

9 sts x 12 rows = 4 in. (10 cm)
Adjust needle size if necessary to obtain gauge.

STITCH GUIDE

Jeny's Stretchy Slipknot Cast-On: This cast-on is like creating one slipknot after another. Start with a slipknot on RH needle. Cast on one stitch with a back-ward loop, lift the top of the loop just cast on up from the needle with a finger and wrap yarn from back to front around needle close to the loop just cast on and pull it through (similar to a crochet chain stitch). Carry the backward loop over the yarn just wrapped, passing the backward loop off the needle. Holding the underside of the cast-on stitch, pull down to tighten. Repeat. This is much easier to understand by watching Jeny's YouTube video: youtube.com/watch?v=3n8E3I6Cg2k.

Stretchy Bind-Off: Bind off first stitch as usual, then: *Yo, k1, pass yo stitch and previous stitch over stitch just knit. Repeat from * to end.

Pick up and purl: Insert needle into stitch from which a new stitch will be made *from the back*, pick up a stitch (as if purling), and pull through from the back.

C4B (cable 4 back): Slip 2 sts onto cable needle and hold to back, k2 from left-hand needle, k2 from cable needle.

C4F (cable 4 front): Slip 2 sts onto cable needle and hold to front, k2 from left-hand needle, k2 from cable needle.

Slipper (Make 2)

CO 18 (22) sts with Jeny's Stretchy Slipknot Cast-On.

Join to knit in the round, being careful not to twist.

Rnd 1: Purl.

Rnd 2: [K1, p1] 5 (7) times, k8.

Rnds 3–4: Rep Rnd 2.

Rnd 5: [K1, p1] 5 (7) times, C4F, C4B.

Rnds 6–8: Rep Rnd 2.

Rnd 9: Rep Rnd 5.

Rnd 10: P10 (14), k8.

Rnd 11: BO 10 (14) sts, k8 (8) sts remaining.

Note: Pattern for both sizes is the same from this point on. Begin knitting back and forth in rows, as follows:

Row 12: Purl.

Row 13: C4F, C4B.

Row 14: Purl.

Row 15: Knit.

Row 16: Purl.

Row 17: C4F, C4B.

Row 18: Purl.

Row 19: Knit.

Row 20: Purl.

Row 21: C4F, C4B.

Row 22: Sl 1, p4, p2tog, turn.
Row 23: Sl 1, k2, k2tog, turn.
Row 24: Sl 1, p2, p2tog, turn.
Row 25: Sl 1, k2, k2tog; *form gusset*: pick up and knit 5 sts on heel flap, turn.
Row 26: P4, k5, pick up and purl 5 sts on heel flap, turn.
Row 27: K4, p6, k4.
Row 28: P4, k6, p4.
Row 29: Ssk, k2, p6, k2, k2tog.
Row 30: P3, k6, p3.
Row 31: Ssk, k1, p6, k1, k2tog.
Row 32: P2, k6, p2.
Row 33: P2tog, k6, p2tog—8 sts.
Row 34: Knit.
Row 35: Purl.

Sole

Rep Rows 34–35 until sole is same as length of foot, ending with a WS row (knit across).

Foot

Row 1 (RS): Sl 1, knit to end, pick up and knit 1, turn.
Row 2: Sl 1, purl to end, pick up and purl 1, turn.
Rep until there is room to pick up 1 more stitch from either side, ending on a WS row.
Before decrease row, count sts and mark middle stitch. *Note:* If, after sl 1 st, remaining stitches are an odd number, mark middle stitch. Stop before marked st, sl 1, k2tog, psso.
Dec row 1: Sl 1, ssk to marker, k2tog to end, pick up and knit stitch from sole.
Dec row 2: Sl 1, [p2tog] twice, purl to last 4 sts, [p2tog] twice, pick up and purl 1 st from sole.
Row 3 (RS): BO all sts—*do not break yarn or finish off*—pick up and knit 1 from bottom stitch of small gusset—2 sts on needle.

Strap

Switch to dpn or circular needle and create I-cord with 2 sts until length fits comfortably over instep of foot. K2tog and cut yarn, pull through remaining stitch. Use tail to fasten strap and attach at bottom of short gusset on other side of slipper.

ROCOCO COWL

Design by Claire Slade

*C*ombining lace stitches with a bulky weight yarn means you can knit an elegant cowl in next to no time. The deeply fluted edging frames the face while the thick yarn warms the neck.

FINISHED MEASUREMENTS

12 in. (30.5 cm) deep x 30 in. (76 cm) circumference, blocked

YARN

Rowan Cocoon; bulky weight #5 yarn; 80% merino wool, 20% kid mohair; 126 yd. (115 m) and 3.5 oz. (100 g) per skein
» 1 skein Misty Blue

NEEDLES AND OTHER MATERIALS

» U.S. size 10 (6 mm) 16 in. (40 cm) circular needle

GAUGE

14 sts in pattern, heavily blocked = 4 in. (10 cm)
Adjust needle size if necessary to obtain gauge.

Cowl

Loosely CO 104 sts and join to work in the round, being careful not to twist.

Purl 1 row.

Repeat the following 6 rounds (either the written or charted instructions) for a total of 7 times, ending on Rnd 6.

Rnd 1: *Ssk, k9, k2tog; rep from * to end of rnd.

Rnd 2: Knit.

Rnd 3: *Ssk, k7, k2tog; rep from * to end of rnd.

Rnd 4: Knit.

Rnd 5: *Ssk, yo, (k1, yo) 5 times, k2tog; rep from * to end of rnd.

Rnd 6: Purl.

Once you have repeated the pattern 7 times, BO loosely as follows: K1, *k1, slip both sts back to the left needle and k2tog tbl; rep from * to end.

Break yarn, thread through the remaining stitch and secure.

Finishing

Soak the cowl in warm water until completely saturated, carefully squeeze out the excess water, then block the cowl to the stated dimensions, pulling the points out at both the top and bottom.

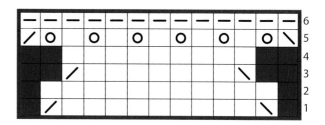

Rococo Cowl Chart

	Knit
—	Purl
/	K2tog
\	SSK
O	Yarn over
■	No stitch
	Repeat

BOBBLE HEADBAND

Design by Tessa Sweigert

tay warm and stylish with this quick headband. With one skein of yarn, you can knit one for yourself and another for a friend! This is an easy project for beginning knitters, too, to show their blossoming skills.

FINISHED MEASUREMENTS

19.5 in. (43 cm) circumference and 3^1/$_2$ in. (9 m) wide

YARN

Loops & Threads Country Loom; super bulky #6 yarn; 100% acrylic; 104 yd. (95 m) and 4.94 oz. (140 g) per skein
  » 1 skein #01201 Ocean Tide

NEEDLES AND OTHER MATERIALS

  » U.S. size 15 (10 mm) knitting needles
  » Tapestry needle

GAUGE

10 sts x 15 rows = 4 in. (10 cm)
Adjust needle size if necessary to obtain gauge.

NOTES

  » Headband is knit flat and seamed.

Headband

CO 48 sts.
Row 1: *P1, k3; rep from * to end of row.
Row 2: *P3, k1; rep from * to end of row.
Row 3: Knit.
Row 4: *P3tog, (k1, p1, k1) in same st; rep from * to end of row.
Row 5: Purl.
Row 6: *(K1, p1, k1) in same st, p3tog; rep from * to end of row.
Row 7: Purl.
Repeat Rows 4–6 one more time.
Repeat Rows 1–2.
BO.

Finishing

Sew ends together, and weave in yarn ends.

WATER BOTTLE COZY

Design by Brenda Castiel

A *great gift for the holidays or all year round—a water bottle carrier to help keep everyone hydrated. Make one in school colors or in a holiday theme to make it special. It's great for hiking or biking, and it absorbs condensation, so you can toss it in a tote bag without worrying about getting things wet. The easy mesh lace pattern expands to fit any size bottle. I-cord provides a sturdy strap.*

FINISHED MEASUREMENTS

6½ in. (16.5 cm) high and 8 in. (20.25 cm) around. It stretches to fit most bottles.

YARN

Solid Color Version (shown): Knit Picks Stroll Sport; fine weight #2 yarn; 75% wool, 25% nylon; 137 yd. (125 m) and 1.7 oz. (50 g) per skein

» 1 skein Rouge *Project usage: approximately 55 yd. (50 m)*

Colorwork Version: Knit Picks Stroll Sport; fine weight #2 yarn; 75% wool, 25% nylon; 137 yd. (125 m) and 1.7 oz. (50 g) per skein

» 1 skein Main Color (MC) *Project usage: approximately 55 yd. (50 m)*
» Small amounts of Contrasting Color(s) (CC)

NEEDLES AND OTHER MATERIALS

» U.S. size 5 (3.75 mm) double-pointed needles, 2 circular needles, or 1 long circular needle (your preference for working in the round)
» Stitch marker
» Tapestry needle

GAUGE

20 sts x 24 rows in St st = 4 in. (10 cm)
Adjust needle size if necessary to obtain gauge.

STITCH GUIDE

S2kp: Slip 2 sts together as if to knit, k1, pass both slipped stitches over knitted st.

Pattern

Loosely CO 40 sts in MC. Join to work in the round, being careful not to twist sts. Pm to indicate beg of round.
Rnd 1: Knit.
Rnd 2: Purl.

Solid Color Version

Rnds 3–12: Rep Rnds 1–2 five more times.
Rnd 13: Knit.

Colorwork Version

Rnds 3–4: Rep Rnds 1–2 once more.
Rnds 5–12 (14): Work according to chosen Motif Chart, knitting all sts in charted colors, repeating motif 5 times each round.
Next Rnd: Using MC, knit.

Both Versions

Rnd 1: Using MC, *k1, yo, s2kp, yo; rep from * to end of rnd.
Rnd 2: Knit.
Rep Rnds 1–2 until piece measures 6 in. (15 cm), lightly stretched, ending with Rnd 2.
Knit 1 rnd.

Decreases

Rnd 1: *K1, yo, s2kp, yo, k1, s2kp; rep from * to end of rnd—30 sts.
Rnd 2: Knit.
Rnd 3: *K1, s2kp, k1; rep from * to end of rnd—18 sts.
Rnd 4: Knit.

Rnd 5: *K2tog, k1; rep from * to end of rnd—12 sts.
BO rem 12 sts.

Finishing

Using dpn or circular needle, pick up and knit 4 sts at CO row for the I-cord strap. *K4, slip the stitches to right end of needle; rep until strap is about 30–35 in. (75–87 cm), lightly stretched. Increase the length if the wearer is taller; note that the bottle's weight will cause the strap to stretch.
Attach I-cord to opposite side of CO row.
Weave in ends.

Motif Charts

Apple Motif

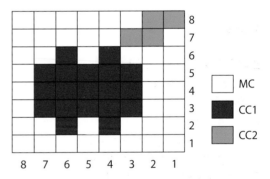

Heart Motif

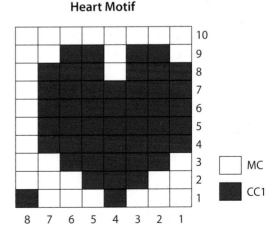

ARCTIC COWL

Design by Anna Smegal

I was inspired to knit this cowl after seeing a similar stitch pattern knit by my great-grandmother. Knit with two strands of thick yarn held together, it is sure to keep you warm even on the coldest of winter days. Six buttons ensure that there are (almost) endless options for style! And, to make the knitting quicker, the relaxed fabric makes it easy to push the buttons through, so no buttonholes need to be knit. Choose either bulky weight yarn or super bulky weight yarn, depending on how cold your arctic weather may turn.

FINISHED MEASUREMENTS

Bulky weight yarn version: 8^1/$_2$ in. (21.5 cm) wide by 27^1/$_2$ in. (70 cm) long

Super bulky weight yarn version: 9^1/$_2$ in. (24 cm) wide by 27^1/$_2$ in. (70 cm) long

YARN

Bulky weight version: Berroco Borealis; bulky weight #5 yarn; 60% acrylic, 40% wool; 108 yd. (100 m) and 3.5 oz. (100 g) per skein

» 2 skeins #5088 Vik

Super bulky weight version: Red-orange sample knit in Bernat Softee Chunky; super bulky weight #6 yarn; 100% acrylic; 108 yd. (99 m) and 3.5 oz. (100 g) per skein

» 2 skeins Redwood

Gold sample knit in Lion Brand Hometown USA; super bulky weight #6 yarn; 100% acrylic; 64 yd. (59 m) and 4 oz. (113 g) per skein

» 3 skeins El Paso Autumn

NEEDLES AND OTHER MATERIALS

» U.S. size 19 (16 mm) knitting needles
» U.S. N (10 mm) crochet hook
» For bulky weight yarn version: Six ^{3}/$_4$ in. (2 cm) buttons
» For super bulky weight yarn version: Six 1^3/$_8$ in. (3.5 cm) buttons
» 36 in. (91 cm) of matching fingering weight yarn for sewing buttons
» Tapestry needle

GAUGE

Bulky weight yarn version: 7 sts x 10 rows in St st, before and after blocking = 4 in. (10 cm)

Super bulky weight yarn version: 6 sts x 9 rows in St st, before and after blocking = 4 in. (10 cm)

Adjust needle size if necessary to obtain gauge.

NOTES

» To work a crochet cast-on: With yarn held double and crochet hook, make slip knot on hook. Hold hook parallel to and on the right side of knitting needle in left hand. Holding yarn in left hand, bring yarn under knitting needle to left, and then bring crochet hook over the knitting needle to catch the yarn and chain one. There should now be one stitch on knitting needle and always one stitch on the crochet hook. Bring yarn back between crochet hook and knitting needle, back under knitting needle to left, and repeat until one stitch less than desired. Slip stitch from hook to knitting needle. For a video tutorial, please refer to Knit Purl Hunter's video "Crochet Cast-On" at knitpurlhunter.com.

» To create a slip-stitch edge, the first stitch of every row is always slipped purlwise. To do this, hold the yarn in front of the work and slip the first stitch as if to purl. Bring the yarn to the back of the work in between the needle tips and work in pattern across row.

Cowl

With yarn held double, CO 16 sts using crochet cast-on.

Row 1 (RS): Sl 1 purlwise wyif, knit to end of row.

Row 2 (WS): Sl 1 purlwise wyif, *k2, p4; rep from * to last 3 sts, k3.

Rep Rows 1–2 until knitting measures $26\frac{1}{2}$ in. (67 cm) from beginning or to desired length, ending after working a Row 2 (WS).

BO. Weave in ends.

Finishing

If desired, block cowl.

Sew buttons on bound-off edge using fingering weight yarn as follows: Align 5 buttons $\frac{1}{2}$ in. (1.3 cm) from the edge, one on each garter and stockinette section. Sew sixth button approximately $3\frac{1}{2}$ in. (8.9 cm) below button on garter strip where last st was bound off.

About Anna Smegal

Anna Smegal learned the basics of knitting from her sister and then taught herself everything else from books. When she isn't catching up on last year's "IOU" Christmas presents, she enjoys knitting projects to enter in the state fair and tech editing other designers' patterns.

*Shown in Berroco Borealis
bulky weight yarn*

*Shown in Bernat Softee Chunky
super bulky weight yarn*

*Shown in Lion Brand
Hometown USA super
bulky weight yarn*

Abbreviations

beg	begin(ing)
BO	bind off
CC	contrasting color
CO	cast on
cn	cable needle
dpn	double-pointed needle(s)
inc	increase(ing)
k	knit
k2tog	knit 2 together
k3tog	knit 3 together
kfb	knit in front and back
LH	left hand
M1	make 1
MC	main color
p	purl
p2tog	purl 2 together
p3tog	purl 3 together
pm	place marker
psso	pass slipped stitch over
rem	remain(ing)
rep	repeat

RH	right hand
rnd	round
RS	right side
s2kp	slip 2 sts together as if to knit, k1, pass both slipped stitches over knitted st
sk2p	slip 1 st knitwise, k2tog, pass slipped stitch over
sl	slip
sm	slip marker
ssk	slip 1 st knitwise, slip the next st knitwise, insert the LH needle into the front leg of both stitches on the RH needle and knit them together
St st	stockinette stitch
st(s)	stitch(es)
tbl	through the back loop
w&t	wrap and turn
WS	wrong side
wyib	with yarn in back
wyif	with yarn in front
yo	yarn over

Contributors

Neisha Abdulla
ravelry.com/people/neish
loveknitting.com/catalogsearch/result/
　　?order=relevance&dir=desc&q=
　　neish+designs

Kath Andrews
ravelry.com/designers/kath-andrews
ravelry.com/people/greenfairy

Vikki Bird
ravelry.com/designers/vikki-bird
vikkibirddesigns.com/
instagram.com/vikki.bird/

Helena Callum
ravelry.com/designers/helena-callum
helenacallum.com

Brenda Castiel
ravelry.com/designers/brenda-castiel
knitandtravelandsuch.blogspot.com
twitter.com/brendacastiel
instagram.com/bcastiel/?hl=en

Christen Comer
ravelry.com/people/crobinator

Candi Derr
ravelry.com/people/bren7na

Dana Gervais
ravelry.com/designers/dana-gervais
facebook.com/DanaGervaisDesigns
instagram.com/knitalot924/
twitter.com/Knitalot924
craftsy.com/search?query=Dana+Gervais&
　　type=&categoryUrl=
loveknitting.com/us/catalogsearch/
　　result/?q=dana+Gervais

Ellen Harvey
ravelry.com/people/miele

Faye Kennington
ravelry.com/designers/faye-kennington

Carolyn Kern
ravelry.com/designers/carolyn-kern
carolynkernknits.blogspot.com
instagram.com/carolyn_kern/

Quenna Lee
ravelry.com/designers/quenna-lee
blissfulbyquenna.com
etsy.com/shop/blissful

Szilvia Linczmaier
facebook.com/sylvidesigns
ravelry.com/designers/szilvia-linczmaier
hu.pinterest.com/SylviDesigns

Michelle May
ravelry.com/designers/michelle-may

Erica Mount
ravelry.com/designers/erica-mount

Kristen Polotsky
ravelry.com/designers/kreopolo
instagram.com/kreopolo/

Sandra Ronca
ravelry.com/designers/sandra-ronca
instagram.com/slouchybee/

Faith Schmidt
ravelry.com/designers/faith-schmidt
DistractedKnits.weebly.com
facebook.com/DistractedKnits
instagram.com/distracted_knits/?hl=en

Claire Slade
ravelry.com/designers/claire-slade
verilyknits.co.uk/
twitter.com/verilyknits
instagram.com/verilyknits/

Anna Smegal
ravelry.com/designers/anna-smegal
facebook.com/aersknits/
instagram.com/aersknits/?hl=en
aersknits.wordpress.com

Sarah Sundermeyer
ravelry.com/designers/sarah-sundermeyer

Tessa Sweigert
ravelry.com/people/TwoFloppyEars

Yarn Sources

Bartlettyarns, Inc.
bartlettyarns.com/

Bernat
yarnspirations.com/bernat

Berroco
berroco.com/

Brown Sheep Company
brownsheep.com/

Cascade Yarns
cascadeyarns.com/

Classic Elite Yarns
classiceliteyarns.com/home.php

Debbie Bliss
debbieblissonline.com/

DMC
dmc-usa.com/

Handmaiden Fine Yarn
handmaiden.ca/

Knit Picks
knitpicks.com/

Koigu
koigu.com/

Libby Summers
libbysummers.co.uk/

Lion Brand Yarn Company
lionbrand.com/

Loops & Threads
michaels.com

Malabrigo
malabrigoyarn.com/

Manos del Uruguay
manos.com.uy/

Mirasol Yarn Collection
mirasol.com.pe/yarn_collection_mirasol

Noro
knittingfever.com/brand/noro/

Red Heart
redheart.com

Rowan
knitrowan.com/